Remembrance for Schools and Communities

Grades 4 to 8

Written by Barbara Brockmann
Illustrated by S&S Learning Materials

About the Author:
Barbara Brockmann teaches for the Ottawa Carleton District School Board and the University of Ottawa. She is a 2002 Recipient of the Governor General's Award for Excellence in Teaching Canadian History. She believes Canadian students of every age deserve to have their heritage and history valued and explored in the classroom. For that reason, she purposefully integrates Canadian culture, context, and history into whatever she teaches.

Copyright © 2010

This publication may be reproduced under licence from Access Copyright, or with the express written permission of On The Mark Press / S&S Learning Materials, or as permitted by law.

All rights are otherwise reserved, and no part of this publication may be reproduced, stored in a retrieval system, or transmitted in any form or by any means, electronic, mechanical, photocopying, scanning, recording or otherwise, except as specifically authorized. "We acknowledge the financial support of the Government of Canada through the Book Publishing Industry Development Program (BPIDP) for this project."

All Rights Reserved
Printed in Canada

Published in the United States by:
On the Mark Press
P.O. Box 433
Clayton, New York
13624
www.onthemarkpress.com

Published in Canada by:
S&S Learning Materials
15 Dairy Avenue
Napanee, Ontario
K7R 1M4
www.sslearning.com

ISBN: 9781554950683

SSC1-45

Why a Play for Remembrance Day?

Every November 11th schools across our country hold Remembrance Day Services. Poems are read, songs are sung, a trumpet is played, and children are exhorted to both remember the tragedy of war and the benefits of peace. But beyond those general concepts, what exactly are they asked to Remember?

Elementary teachers are often uncomfortable teaching the history of Canada's war efforts because of the horrors invariably connected with warfare. Some have little general or specific knowledge of Canada's participation in wars -- due, in part, to the fact that the eras of WWI, WWII, and the Korean War are not usually part of the Grade 1 to Grade 8 curricula across Canada.

Every year teachers scramble to reinvent the Remembrance Day "wheel". And every year the focus is on the 'Poppy', 'Sacrifice,' and 'Peace.' In schools with new immigrant populations, teachers sometimes emphasize current events and the wish for peace in some of their students' conflict laden countries of origin. While this is a well intentioned approach to a difficult subject, it overlooks the rich and moving history of Canada's unique experience of war.

Recognizing these challenges we must remember that there is one day a year – in fact one hour of that one day – where educators across the country have the opportunity of helping younger students develop a meaningful understanding of how the experience of War has played an integral part in painting the canvas of Canadian life.

Remembrance Day Plays for Schools and Communities is an **age-appropriate** platform that allows educators to transform this brief yet emotional observance into an imaginative experience of Canada's proud wartime history. While recognizing the sadness and sacrifices of war, these plays honour the bravery and the triumphs of our fallen and our Veterans, their experiences and the experiences of their families and communities.

Theatre serves as a particularly powerful teaching/learning tool. Not only do actors, singers, and dancers directly engage in specific 'roles' within the context of wartime events, an audience of children, parents, and veterans witness a synopsis of the conflict and its social and cultural effects. The past comes alive. What has been especially gratifying is the response of veterans who see children re-enacting and honouring their experiences.

"This has been a great tribute for us veterans, because it brings home our experiences. My father was in the first war, and I was in the second. Now my grandchildren will understand." – Veteran Patrick O'Keeffe.

"I'll tell the Korean War Vets that the Korean War isn't forgotten any longer." – Veteran Les Peate, President of the Korea Veterans Association of Canada.

ISBN: 9781554950683

Table of Contents

Why a Play for Remembrance Day?... 2

Teacher's Guide 4

Making it Work for You 4

Audition Application 4

Dramatic Skills 5

Costumes, Props and Sets 6

Staging Your Production 6

The Ceremony of Remembrance 8

Reflections on my Learning 9

Double Use Rubric 10

PLAY: LETTERS FROM THE GREAT WAR, 1914-1918 (Grades 6 to 8)................ 11

PLAY: WAITING FOR D-DAY, 1939-1945 (Grades 4 to 8) 29

PLAY: REMEMBERING KOREA, 1950-1953 9 (Grades 6 to 8) 48

PLAY: A TRIO OF WARS, A GIFT OF PEACE (Grades 4 to 8) 68

PLAY: FOUR QUESTIONS ABOUT PEACE (Grades 4 to 8) 92

Classroom and Research Bibliography 118

Acknowledgements 120

Ceremony of Remembrance

ISBN: 9781554950683

3

SSC1-45

Teacher's Guide

Making It Work For You:

- Share the directorial talents around! Invite colleagues to take on an aspect of directing (choir or dance) and production (costumes, sound or set construction). Past productions have included primary teachers with classroom choirs, and a Grade 8 gym teacher directing a 'jive dance' scene. Talented students with dance training have done their own choreography, while students in cadet bands have added military drumbeats. Be flexible with the script and open to the hidden talents of your students and staff.

- Consider the population of students with whom you will stage the play. By using only your own class or only one grade level (all the Grade 6's for example) you may be able to use class time for rehearsals and evaluate performances for a drama mark. In this way you might want to integrate the play's content with a social studies or a language arts unit. On the other hand, if you choose to do the play on a school wide basis – which will require extra-curricular time – this will allow a broader group of students to become involved. In addition, the autumn is a good time to stage a production while meeting the needs of the school to have a memorable Remembrance Day Ceremony.

- Auditions allow you to view the range of student talents and shows prospective actors that a production requires commitment

Auditions: Round One:

It is possible to audition about 30 students over the lunch hour. Students fill out an 'Audition Card' as part of the process. This simply adds a 'gravitas' to the proceedings, but also gives information on background experience.

Audition Application

Name: _____   Grade: _____

1. Have you ever performed in front of an audience before? Briefly describe it:
   _____
   _____
   _____

2. What is your experience with drama, both in AND outside of school?
   _____
   _____
   _____

3. Circle the types of positions you are interested in:

       Acting speaking role   Backstage Crew

       Acting non-speaking role   Sound Crew

       Choir   Dance

       Production Crew (program, front of house, sets)

At the audition, students are given a choice of a scenario that might be found in the play. For example: a brother and sister are having a squabble; a grandparent is complimenting the other grandparent who is at a domestic task; a nurse is tending to a wounded soldier; two soldiers are talking of home before heading out on night patrol. Emphasize use of mime, voice projection, and remembering to face the audience. In pairs, students have five to ten minutes to prepare a one to two minute skit. During their presentations, look especially for body movement and character interpretation, skills which are more complex to teach. Keep three piles of audition slips: Definitely / Shows Promise / Consider for Group Scene.

Auditions: Round Two:

These auditions involve 'call backs' as you start to place students in specific roles. Actors are put in groups and given selections from the script. At this stage you are looking for group dynamics, physical attributes, as well as personal interpretation of characters. Once the final cast selections are in place, rehearsals can begin.

Generally, these plays are written to allow for the use of a maximum number of student actors: crowd scenes really are crowds! In this way, no student is ever 'cut' from the production if they really want to participate.

Dramatic Skills

- Emphasize the **ensemble nature of theatre** where everyone's efforts to make the story 'live' on stage has equal value. Affirm that **there are no small roles, only small actors**.

- Teach **key dramatic skills** to all your actors. These include: **tableau structure** (both interesting body posture and effective freeze); **effective body movement; consistent blocking that avoids upstaging the other actors**; loud, slow and clear **voice projection; fully facing the audience when it's time to talk** (even if in a conversation with another character). These are the skills that will lift your production to a higher level and allow the story to come through.

- **Voice projection is the most important dramatic skill**. Despite the increasing use of hanging and clip on microphones, skills like **enunciation, pacing of speech,** and **loud voice projection** are critically important. Loudness and a good pace tend to go hand in hand: it's hard to speak both loud and fast. Use voice exercises. Build up awareness of who has a good voice in your cast, and how they do it – then use them as a model to improve everyone's projection and enunciation.

- Tell students of the **difference** in your **role** as a **'teacher'** and your role as a **'director'**. Being a director means you will be giving explicit directions – like a sports coach, instead of gentle suggestions – like a teacher! This means that when working with one group, others in the scene are expected to pay attention and listen, as the directions will likely impact their performances too! It also means they can learn from each other's strengths. Making this clear at the beginning of the process lets your budding actors know to what they can expect, adds to the creative experience, and saves hurt feelings (theirs) and frazzled nerves (yours).

- Acting is like writing: it requires changes in each 'draft' as the process unfolds, until the role reveals exactly what the director and the actors mean.

Costumes, Props and Sets

- **Costumes** can be easily put together by using a variety of clothing styles that are available in second hand shops and peoples' closets. Use internet research to get the 'feel' of clothing styles from different eras. Choose simple footwear in neutral colours and avoid neon brights in sneakers.

- **Soldiers' Costumes:** Army and Navy Surplus stores, local museums, Cadet organizations, local collectors, parents, the Legion or local Veterans organizations may be a source of costumes or authentic props. The Canadian War Museum presently has a program to borrow materials called, 'Living History'. Another approach is to start with any Khaki clothing, easily available in second hand stores and family closets and add dimensions of costume which are particular to each era (see chart). Plastic helmets can often be purchased cheaply in dollar or toy stores. Soldier's foot wear should be one colour boots. In previous productions, students have used a key piece of clothing or equipment, like a gas mask or kit bag, which belonged to a relative and have been lovingly passed down.

World War I	World War II	Korean War	Peacekeepers
• heavy wool clothing; jackets are over the hip	• heavy wool clothing in a different style than WWI: jackets were like waist length bomber jackets	• soldiers wore same uniforms as WWII	• have started wearing camouflage styles
• calves wrapped in khaki bandages called 'putees'	• WWII style helmets	• heavily laden down with provisions and knapsacks	• outfits would depend on the climate of the location
• shirts tucked in	• knapsacks or kit bags filled with newspaper	• winter gear	• peacekeepers wear signature light blue baseball caps with UN insignia
• broad WWI helmets			
• props: sandbags made of burlap and stuffed with newspaper			

- **Guns as Props:** The dilemma: Boys like to use 'toy guns', while teachers feel nervous with guns of any kind in a school setting. You can have a supply of simple wooden guns made from a single template and add to your collection as the need arises. You can even use heavy cardboard painted appropriately. The golden rule for actors with prop guns is that they are never pointed towards the audience and are always pointed up high or down low.

- **Keep sets simple.** These plays are usually staged on minimal sets with props that are readily available or easily manufactured.

Staging Your Production

- **Use all available entrances and exits both on and off the stage in the performance area.** Keep things exciting by having the actors, especially the soldiers, go through the audience 'on patrol' and out of alternate exits. This is effective during the War Front scenes and has proven one of the main reasons many boys come out for the production!

- **Music** is a critical part of your production. It has power to communicate an era, a mood, an emotion or an idea. Suggestions for choral pieces connected to specific eras are included within the plays. Many teachers have favourite choral pieces about war and peace which you may substitute or students might have ideas for current tunes with appropriate lyrics. As well, film soundtracks hold great possibility for instrumental mood enhancers, as background to the soldiers on patrol or as musical interludes to set a tone between scenes. Some of my long time favourites are the soundtracks from: Master and Commander, Saving Private Ryan, and Titanic.

- **Programs** help the audience understand the format of the event and provide a nice keepsake for the performers and their parents. Programs can be double sided on 8.5" x 14" paper, folded in half and usually feature the following:
  - Title page with a drawing by a student(s) on the theme of the play and the author's name, as well as production dates and directors.
  - List of scenes, including choir and dance numbers and the Ceremony of Remembrance.
  - A list of the cast, crew, choir and dancers, by classroom, by order of appearance, or alphabetically.
  - Acknowledgements, especially of the Veterans and their families as well as helpful parent volunteers, school staff or community suppliers.

- **Time requirements to stage production** depend on your personal preference as a director. With willing performers and a sharing of directorial roles between choir, dance, and drama, it is possible to stage a production in a shorter, more intense, period of between three to four weeks. Each joint play and ceremony generally runs between 50 to 70 minutes.

Choose students who are organized and observant to run lights and sound. They will need to know their cues and be prepared to meet them.

- Consider doing multiple performances. While these plays are primarily meant to provide a memorable Remembrance Day observance for your school, they can be staged for a wider audience. For example, consider a performance before November 11 for other schools or residents of a local Seniors Home, and for the community on the evening of Remembrance Day. Save the main November 11 performance for your own school; starting at 10:00 a.m. and aiming for an approximate 11 o'clock conclusion.

- If you need to cover your costs, collect donations or charge a nominal fee at public performances. You might even consider donating your fees to a worthy charity for the families of Canadian Soldiers, or to an international charity helping children who are victims of war like War child, or Free the Children.

Letters from the Great War: Scene 4: The Hospital

The Ceremony of Remembrance

The Ceremony of Remembrance follows much the same format for each play. This creates a sense of ritual over the years, and makes a link from the historical era of the play to the same reflective moment of remembrance.

Aspects of the ceremony include:

- **A Gravestone:**

To make one, begin by Googling the internet under "Commonwealth War Graves Commission" (images) to get the correct image of the maple leaf used. Using acrylic paint on thick Styrofoam (a mix of yellow and black makes an effective khaki green colour) paint the maple leaf and "Lest We Forget / Nous nous souvenons" beneath. Due to the multi-faith nature many school environments, do not add the image of the Christian cross. (Note: An inexpensive source of Styrofoam in the right size and shape of a gravestone is sale-priced Halloween cemetery props! Cover the gruesome Halloween side with brown paper, and use the flat surface of the back for your Gravestone.)

- **The Format:**

Curtains open to reveal the gravestone in the centre and four actors evenly spaced with two on each side across the front of the stage. The actors speak their lines. Once they say "We remember and we say thank you," the *Honour March* begins. Music, which is solemn but powerfully moving - like *"Hymn to the Fallen"* from the movie *"Saving Private Ryan"* – is played. The entire cast and crew enter the stage in a dignified and gracious manner four at a time. They walk straight across the back wall of the stage from the wings. They turn sharply towards the audience and walk slowly forward to line up behind the front four actors flanking the headstone. When all of the cast and crew are quietly on stage, making four long lines of performers still in costume, the last person to enter walks up the centre to lay the wreath in front of the gravestone. This may be a Veteran, a student with a personally meaningful connection to the era of the play, or an actor playing a key family or soldier role. Once the wreath is laid that student says

"PLEASE STAND".

It is followed by:

- **BUGLE CALL:** The Last Post

- **MOMENT OF SILENCE**

- The Moment of Silence is ended when the wreath-layer says, **"Please join us in the singing of 'O Canada'."**

- **All sing "O Canada"**

- **Curtains close.** The performance and Ceremony of Remembrance is ended.

Reflections on My Learning

Name: _____   Date: _____

A description of my role or involvement in the production:

_____
_____
_____

The aspect I found most challenging was _____
_____

I met this challenge by _____
_____

Something I can now do with more confidence is _____
because _____

Something that really surprised me was _____
because _____

The part I enjoyed doing the most was _____
because _____

Overall, when I look at this experience, the areas I have shown the most growth in are:

1. _____
   _____

2. _____
   _____

Finally, three ideas or facts that I have learned about war and peace from this play are:

1. _____
   _____

2. _____
   _____

3. _____
   _____

Double-Use Rubric
Student Self-Assessment / Teacher Evaluation

Name: _____   Date: _____

Student Self-Assessment: _____	Teacher Evaluation: _____
Do it first. Use a pencil. Check where you think your skill level is. Afterwards, compare your personal self-assessment to your teacher's evaluation.	*Do it second. Use a coloured pen. Check off your evaluation of the student skill level. You may use the open space to add additional comments.*

Criteria	Level 4: Demonstrates the required criteria in a fluent and compelling manner	Level 3: Demonstrates the required criteria in a proficient and fairly consistent manner	Level 2: Demonstrates the required criteria adequately, but inconsistently	Level 1: Developing the required criteria, or demonstrates them to a limited degree
Learning Skills: Ability to use the following elements and conventions of drama to communicate: • frozen and interesting tableau • body language • loud voice • maintains full frontal facial position when speaking • establishes and maintains a dramatic presence				
Learning Skills: • ability to take and use direction • personal engagement in being prepared for role • appropriate backstage behaviour				

Compare your self-assessment with your teacher's evaluation.

_____
_____
_____

LETTERS FROM THE GREAT WAR: 1914-1918

A Play and A Ceremony

Suitable for Performance by: Grades 6 to 8

Plot Summary:

The play opens in **Scene One: The Call** in a town square somewhere in Canada where young Canadians in three separate groupings announce their intention of 'joining up.' They are: youthful scholar Michael, determined Black Canadian Jeremiah Jones, and spirited Grace MacPherson. In trying to convince a loved one they are doing the 'right thing,' they each promise to write home. As they join the enlistment line, the choir in the town square sings "It's a Long Way to Tipperary."

The "I'll write home as often as I can" theme provides the structure for the rest of the play, in which the characters deliver their 'letters' in a series of interconnected monologues, highlighting and personalizing different aspects of the war experience. The setting is indicated by the scene title. The three young Canadians who were introduced in Scene 1 are integrated throughout the play. **Scene 2: The Trenches** ends in a modern dance entitled "No Man's Land Waltz." **Scene 3: The Munitions Factory at The Home Front** concludes with the singing of "Till the Boys Come Home "(Keep the Home Fires Burning). Michael, Jeremiah, and Grace meet up in **Scene 4: The Hospital**, which ends with a moving choral rendition of "In Flanders Fields."

Michael, Jeremiah, Grace, and Soldier Talbot Papineau lead **Scene 5: Ceremony of Remembrance**. The Cast and Crew enter the stage during the Honour March to solemn but moving music. The laying of the wreathe is followed by the Last Post and the Moment of Silence, which ends with the singing of "O Canada."

Acting Roles:

Speaking roles: 34 individual roles

Group scenes for additional non-speaking roles:
- marketplace opening
- soldiers in the trenches
- munitions factory workers
- wounded soldiers / working nurses in the hospital

Music / Choral Options:

a) *"It's a Long Way to Tipperary"* by Jack Judge and Harry Williams
b) *"Till the Boys Come Home (Keep the Home Fires Burning)"* by Lena Guilbert Ford and Ivor Novello
c) *"In Flander's Fields"* by Lieutenant-Colonel John McCrae. (Many musical versions are available.)
d) Honour March: *"Hymn to the Fallen"* from the movie "*Saving Private Ryan*"

Dance Options:

"No Man's Land Waltz": a modern dance to jolting or haunting instrumental music which emphasizes the madness of trench warfare, and the tragedy of this war in particular.

[Previous performances: Fisher Park Public and Summit Alternative Public School, Ottawa, Ontario]
[Directed by Barbara Brockmann (2002) and Dale Hayward (2004, 2006, 2008)]

ISBN: 9781554950683

Characters and Costumes

In order of appearance. Roles with full names are based on real people.
Use the character list below to record the names of your cast members!

Scene 1: *The Call*

Michael: (*young, scholarly, enthusiastic*) _____

Father: (*older, distinguished*) _____

Jeremiah Jones: (*determined, Black Canadian, dressed for a church picnic*) _____

Marie: (*Black Canadian girlfriend, dressed for a church picnic*) _____

Grace MacPherson: (*20 years old, spirited, intelligent*) _____

Mother: (*older woman*) _____

Non Speaking Roles: (*two enlistment officers, various people in a crowd*) _____
_____

The Choir: (*could be dressed in 1910's clothing with appropriate hats or caps and perform onstage like an era-appropriate choral group*)

Scene 2: *The Trenches*

Group A: (*relates to early war experience, tone is generally teasing and information is presented slightly ironically, still with a sense of humour*)

Soldier 1: <u>Robert Dorman:</u> (*very young and naive*) _____

Soldier 2: (*describes experience of waiting and the trenches*) _____

Soldier 3: (*describes trench foot*) _____

Soldier 4: (*emphasizes noise*) _____

Soldier 5: (*camaraderie among the varied "boys"*) _____

Soldier 6: (*darkly descriptive forays into no-man's land*) _____

Group B: (*relates to experiences of critical Canadian battles*)

Soldier 7: <u>Michael</u>: (*Ypres and the gas experience*) _____

Soldier 8: (*the Somme*) _____

Soldier 9: (*victory at Vimy*) _____

Soldier 10: <u>Jeremiah Jones</u>: (*victory at Vimy*) _____

Soldier 11: <u>Brigadier General Alex Ross</u>: (*victory at Vimy*) _____

Group C: (*tone is tired and disheartened*)

Soldier 12: <u>Francis Pegahmagabow</u>: (*Aboriginal Canadian, serious, deliberate*) _____

Soldier 13: (*angry about the war*) _____

Soldier 14: <u>Talbot Papineau</u>: (*questions the war*) _____

Soldier 15: (*weary, full of premonition, mentions Paschendaele*) _____

Non-Speaking Roles: (*this scene may make use of additional soldiers*) _____

Scene 3: *Munitions Factory at The Home Front*

The munitions workers are wearing period skirts and blouses underneath matching simple grey or blue cotton tunics. Hair is tied up under unadorned shower caps. They may mime or carry a variety of items like a pail, hammer, screwdriver, or a large funnel.

Munitions Worker 1: (*rough girl*) _____

Munitions Worker 2: (*rich, middle aged, secretly pleased*) _____

Munitions Worker 3: (*middle class wife, worried*) _____

Munitions Worker 4: (*hard working, former servant, very capable*) _____

Munitions Worker 5: (*young, university student*) _____

Munitions Worker 6: (*Michael's sister*) _____

Munitions Worker 7: (*working class*) _____

Munitions Worker 8: (<u>*Marie*</u> - *same as Scene 1*) _____

Non-Speaking Roles: (*Additional female factory workers: enough to make lines of factory workers on the stage, out of which the actresses emerge.*)

_____

_____

Scene 4: *The Hospital*

Nurses were called "bluebirds" and wore a light blue blouses with blue A-line skirts. This outfit had a starched white collar and white cuffs. Doctors might be dressed in army uniforms with white jackets on top. Stretcher bearers would be dressed in army uniforms and wearing Red Cross armbands. There would be several soldiers wearing uniforms with parts of their bodies bandaged, or lying in bed in pyjamas.

Nurse 1: (*bluebird uniform, harried*) _____

Grace: (*dirty and blood stained mechanics overalls, cap*) _____

Soldier 10: (*Jeremiah - in bed with pyjama's and housecoat, bandaged shoulder*) _____

Stretcher Bearer 1: (*working class man, appealing to God*) _____

Stretcher Bearer 2: (*working class man, quietly heroic*) _____

Nurse 2: (*bluebird uniform, thoughtful*) _____

Patient 1: (*philosophical*) _____

Patient 2: (*Black Canadian*) _____

Lieutenant Colonel Doctor John McCrae: (*frustrated, begging*) _____

Nurse 4: Marion Landry: (*bluebird uniform, thoughtful, mature*) _____

Non-Speaking Roles: *Soldiers wrapped in bandages, or being bandaged. Some resting, talking, playing cards. Could use the same soldiers as in Scene 2.*

_____

_____

SCENE 1: *THE CALL*

Golden light floods the stage while popular period music plays and a crowd mingles in the town square. A table and two chairs are carried out and used by two officers while a third soldier flanks a large "ENLIST NOW" sign. Out of the crowd emerges three distinct groupings: Michael and his Father, Jeremiah and Marie, Grace and her Mother. Freeze into tableaus.

Father: Michael, what's the meaning of that uniform? Where are your school books?

Michael: Since war has been declared Father, my plans have changed. I've signed up.

Father: (*stunned*) What do you mean you've signed up? How could you?

Michael: Actually, father, the question is really more like: How could I NOT sign up when my country needs me? I wouldn't be able to live with myself if I didn't do my bit. University will just have to wait.

Father: Of course I don't want you to go, but frankly, I understand your feelings. If I was a young man again I'd probably do the same thing. Your mother though (*shakes head*)… convincing her will be another matter.

Michael: Everyone's saying we'll be home by Christmas. (*gets an idea*) Perhaps I'll stay on a bit longer once it's over. I could tour around Europe. Maybe visit the old sod and see where you and Mother were born. (*emphasis*) And no matter what, I'll be sure to write to you everyday!

Father claps Michael on the back and they freeze

Jeremiah: (*Looking into the picnic basket and smacking his lips.*) What a fine picnic you've prepared Marie.

Marie: (*coyly*) I had an idea you'd pick my basket at the church harvest fair.

Jeremiah: (*teasing her*) Well, after you told me that the one with the yellow bow had your fried chicken and raspberry pie, I knew what to do!

Marie: Why Jeremiah Jones, aren't you the boldest thing. (*pouting*) Maybe next church picnic I'll tell Austin Davis which basket is mine.

Jeremiah: (*becoming serious*) You just might have to do that anyway Marie. You see, I've decided to enlist.

Marie: Jeremiah! What did you want to go and do that for? What has the government ever done for you or for our families?

Jeremiah: I know Marie, but this is not about what the government has or hasn't done for us. This is a war and like all the other boys I have to do my bit to protect you and our families. Besides, I'm certain that after we do our part the government will give us some part in running the government! They need us Marie. Just last week, Albert tried to enlist but they turned him down on the basis of his skin colour. Phhhhh! The government may think they don't need us yet, but they will. And when that time comes, I'll be going.

(*Marie becomes teary and turns away.*)

Jeremiah: (*moving close to Marie*) And, Marie, while I'm away, will you write to me... everyday?

Puts arm around her, and they freeze.

Grace: Momma, I simply must go. You KNOW that I was the first girl in Vancouver to have my own car. You KNOW I can fix my own automobile and change my own tires. Just last week I had a blow out, I jacked up the car and changed the tire all by myself.

Momma: Gracie, I admit you are talented behind the wheel. But driving around town is not the same thing as going off to war.

Grace: Well, how about when that silly teenage boy ran in front of my car and got himself knocked down? I kept my cool. I was decisive. I knew every second counted and so I put him in my car and drove him right to the hospital. I did what needed to be done when it needed to be done. I didn't scream or go into hysterics like some nervous Nelly. Even the police praised my quick thinking.

Momma: Even so Gracie, you're the youngest of my children, and with your brother Alex so recently killed at Gallipoli (*chokes up*)...

Grace: Don't you see Mother, that's exactly why I must go. I also never dreamed that Alex would die. He was always so lucky. And now that I've just heard that Boy Templeton was killed in action I am more certain than ever that this is what I must do. I'm sure I could be an ambulance driver and once I'm there the willpower and courage will come to me.

Momma: An ambulance driver? Whoever would let a girl drive an ambulance?

Grace: The Volunteer Aid Detachment. They need the boys for fighting and they need us girls for everything else.

Momma: But...but...How will you ever travel from here in Vancouver to Europe?

Grace: I...I didn't want to let you in on this until I had a definite plan, but I've been going to the Canadian Pacific Steamship Office every day at lunch for the past two months asking for free passage. I told them. "The boys get it, why not me? I'm volunteering too." And they gave it to me Mum: free passage to England. I leave next Thursday.

Momma: Gracie, my Grace... (*They embrace*) I'll only let you go if you promise to write home as often as possible.

Grace embraces her mother. The crowd becomes animated again as the three young people join the line-up. Choral group moves to the lip of the stage as curtains close behind them.

CHOIR: "*It's A Long Way to Tipperary,*" by Jack Judge and Harry Williams

SCENE 2: *THE TRENCHES*

The soldiers pour into the theatre space through any available doors, moving low and quickly, as if on patrol. Once on stage they take up position in their groups A, B, or C. Ominous music plays. Each group rotates to centre front where they have their moment in the spotlight when the music stops and the side groups freeze in tableau. Each location has its own distinct task: soldiers stage right might be hunched over a small fire warming their hands or making tea; soldiers centre stage where the performance takes place are writing and reading; soldiers stage left are sniping or preparing to go "over the top."

<u>Group A</u>: letters relate to early war experience, information is initially presented with an ironic but humourous or teasing tone.

Soldier 1: *Robert Dorman:* Dear Mother, it's your own Bob with the 75th division of the Canadian Expeditionary Force. I can hardly believe I'm actually here in uniform, especially after you yanked me out the first time I enlisted on account of me being underage. I understand why you did it Mother, but I need you to understand why I had to sneak away to join up. So here it is: a little "Verse And Worse" by R.O. Bob Dorman. I called it "The Argument".

> Hello Mother, what do you know
> I enlisted today I said I'd go
> Yes, I mean to do my little bit
> Afraid? Why Mum, never thought of it
> Oh I know it's true all that you say
> Only fifteen and going away
> But age don't count it's the heart within
> The courage to lose the faith to win
> So come now Mother, you mustn't cry
> Other boys have joined so why not I
> It won't last long please understand
> Then I'll come Home to the things we planned

> Remember Mum, what you have often said
> *The little house all painted red* (emphasis)
> A garden filled with lovely flowers
> Where we planned to spend such happy hours
> I know how much it all means to you dear
> But really I couldn't be happy there
> When I know that every Mother's son
> Is badly needed to man the guns
> So cheer up Mother don't take it so hard
> You wouldn't have your son branded a coward
> Come smile thru your tears and think of the day
> When I'll return Home to be with you always.

(*Acknowledgement of poem from Robert Dorman at www.pastvoices.com/canada*)

Soldier 2: Hey Sis, You won't believe this, but we are living in ditches. I kid you not! Long lines of ditches dug into the ground, sandbagged on top, with rows of barbed wire just beyond for extra protection from marauding Germans. They call them "trenches." When I signed up, I pictured myself a glorious and brave cavalry officer mounted on the back of a dashing steed, bravely facing the enemy in an all out charge, like in my boyhood games. Instead, here I am wrapped in a heavy wool uniform, wearing a tin hat, and sitting under a muddy rain-proof sheet – sitting, cooking, eating, sleeping, standing too, and wading through mud. Sometimes shooting and being shot at. Always being shelled. But going, it seems, nowhere.

Soldier 3: Dear Mrs. O'Keeffe, Many thanks to you and the ladies of the Women's Church Auxiliary for knitting us those warm woollen socks. I cannot express to you enough the gratitude myself and the boys feel when we pull them on. Standing in open trenches we often find ourselves with our feet in several inches of water. When your feet are sitting wet for any length of time, you know how the skin pickles and gets soft and bumpy. Here, the worst cases are called "trench foot," and those with it…well, their feet simply rot away. Sorry, I don't mean to shock you or the rest of the very kind Church ladies. Our Officers have it as a standing order that we have to change our socks every day. And it's not as if we're lazy – it's simply impossible to keep our feet dry. However, your new socks make that a lot easier. And Mrs. O'Keeffe, please send my kindest regards to your daughter Kathleen. She'll remember me from Queen Victoria High School. Please tell her I would be delighted if she consented to commence a correspondence with me. And that way I'll be able to let you know how my feet are doing in my new woollen socks!

Soldier 4: Samuel my son, you shouldn't rush your schooling at the Music Conservatory to join the Canadian Expeditionary Force. You – who loves music above all else – would go mad at the constant shelling. It affects even the strongest of us. The noise and the shaking of the earth gives us the most dreadful headaches and turns us deaf. And there is nothing we can do, except sit in torment and wait for it to finish. I try to drown it out by humming Beethoven's Ninth Symphony in my head but nothing calms my nerves. (*covers ears, and starts to hum*)

Soldier 5: Dear Mum, You don't have to worry about me. I am here in good company. I couldn't hope to meet a better bunch of fellows. And what a grand, mixed lot we are. There are fruit farmers, and loggers, and bank managers in our battalion – you name it. And we joined up pretty much to the man because we want to do our duty. These are the sort of fellows you can rely on no matter what happens. And for that I am very grateful. In the meantime, please tell Leo he'll have to get another hired man for the spring planting. The way things look now there's no chance I'll be home by then. Signing off, your loving son, Ralph.

Soldier 6: Dear Madeline, It's evening here at the front. Last night I was sent out on a sortie into no-man's land. "No man's land" – what's that you ask? I can see you shaking your gorgeous curls. Don't let that name fool you my dear – no man's land is full of men, dead ones, that is. It's what they call the muddy, rotting, stinking stretch of craters between our trenches and the enemy. Every night it comes alive as we're sent out in small parties to bring something back, whether that "something" is information, German prisoners, or our own wounded. First, we have to inch through the barbed wire. Then, we crawl like rats from shell-hole to shell-hole, hugging the ground. When a flare arches up we stop dead still and pray no one can tell us from the mud. Every little hill, bump or pile of sludge is like a mountain to us. Many's the time I have lain out there – stock-still – just thinking of you. It's what gets me through.

Group B: *Letters relate to critical Canadian battles. The tone should be emotional and the acting is animated.*

Soldier 7: *Michael:* Dear Father. Finally, News you can be proud of! We were in Ypres for only a week this April 1915 when our first stretch of fighting began. At dawn, strange green clouds of gas floated across the fields from the German lines. We heard about this from the African troops we relieved. The green clouds covered the trenches directly to our left, where the French soldiers were. They ran from their positions in a panic and left the line open to the Germans. We held our line and counterattacked with a fierceness that surprised the enemy; thankfully they did not advance. But again the green clouds floated across no-man's land, but this time in our direction. Our boys in the Princess Pat's bore the brunt of the attack. Chlorine gas. Chemical weapons used against people. With horrible results. This is the first time poison gas has been used in any war. Some of our guys figured out if you peed in your handkerchief and held it over your nose and mouth it would give you some protection. (*Soldiers around him start to cough and gasp, pull out white handkerchiefs and cover their mouths and noses.*) Not the kind of thing you'd want to do on a regular basis you understand, but that trick saved our lives. We Canadians held that line until we were relieved. We held that line, despite our loses of over 6,000 men, a full third of our forces in this battle. (*Almost cries, then straightens out*). We held that line, and we made a name for the Canadians. From what I've heard, they're saying we averted a full scale disaster.

Soldier 8: Dear Johnny, The news is in. Even for us, who you'd think would be used to death by now, it's devastating. You remember Eileen's cousin, Owen Steele, who was in the Newfoundland Regiment? I saw him just a few weeks ago when we were on leave. We had a few laughs and he was telling me about the immense preparations being made for "the Big Push" on the Somme. He said that roads in every direction were packed with wagons and troops for miles and miles and he was sure victory would follow. I know he was one of the 801 soldiers of the Regiment who went over the top at Beaumont Hamel on July 1, but the question is was he one of only the 68 who survived. Can you believe it? 733 men killed or wounded in less than half an hour. An entire generation of young men slaughtered. I am sure all of Newfoundland is weeping, and we are weeping with them.

Soldier 9 and 10 Jeremiah Jones stand "back to back" as their monologues tell of the same battle.

Soldier 9: Dear Ma, At last! We did it! We took back some ground from the Germans. And Jeremiah Jones and I were part of it!

Soldier 10: *Jermiah:* Like I was telling you in my letters, Marie, for more than two years the Germans occupied Vimy Ridge and no one could move them. Until us that is! Three cheers for General Arthur Currie, the first Canadian born general to lead us into battle.

Soldier 9: General Currie left nothing to chance, and planned the attack on Vimy Ridge down to the last detail. He used aeroplanes to take photographs of the German defences. Then our commanders constructed a huge model of the German emplacements so we knew where every trench, machine gun nest, and communication centre was.

Soldier 10: *Jeremiah:* They even gave us blokes maps so we could study the lay of the land. Not only that, we rehearsed our exact plans of attack. I knew precisely where I was going when I went over the top! I cleared out a German dug out and captured the survivors and their machine gun. Right according to plan!

Soldier 9: Tell Jeremiah's mum that from what I saw he should get a Distinguished Conduct Medal. I was wounded shortly after the battle began and they sent me back to England. There was a great crowd of people at the dock when our hospital ship came in. Just as we were landing somebody in the crowd shouts. "The Canadians! The Canadians! They've taken Vimy Ridge! They taken Vimy "Bloody Ridge." And then what a cheer went up! They threw chocolate bars. They threw flowers. In fact, I broke down and cried.

Soldier 10: *Jeremiah:* We achieved something many said was impossible. It was the first real allied victory of the War. I think myself that it was at Vimy Ridge that Canada was born.

(*Soldiers 9 and 10 stand to attention and then put their arms over each others shoulders in a brotherly fashion.*)

Soldier 11: *Brigadier General Alex Ross:* Dear Lord Beaverbrook, You have asked me to send my recollections about the Victory at Vimy to the Canadian War Office. What I can recall is that at zero hour, the barren earth erupted humanity. From dugouts, shell holes, and trenches men sprang into action, fell into artillery formations, and advanced to the ridge, every division of the Corps moved forward together. It was Canada from the Atlantic to the Pacific on parade. I thought then, and I think today, that in those few minutes I witnessed the birth of a nation.

<u>Group C:</u> Letters relate to later war experience. Tone is tired and disheartened.

Soldier 12: *Francis Pegahmagabow:* Dear Chief and Members of the Parry Island Band, Thank you for the warm blankets, the tobacco and chocolate. They are much appreciated here and I have shared them with my fellow soldiers. You asked for verification of the news you have received from my company commander. My fellow soldiers call me "Peggy," and I am known for my sniping skills, and my ability to slip behind enemy lines. It is true I have captured over 250 enemy soldiers so far. Many thanks for your acknowledgement of my third bar for bravery. You would have all done the same. I look forward to returning home and living in harmony with this world. Sincerely, Francis Pegahmagabow.

Scene 2: The Trenches

Soldier 13: Dear Journal, I promised I would write only the truth on your pages. One truth that cannot be captured on your pages, thankfully, is the stench of death. It envelopes every waking moment. You feel terrible for every mother's son lying in the field in front and all around us. If only the mothers realized what their babes have come to, they would storm the Generals' offices and never let them order another advance. They would shake the politicians until they talked out whatever silly insult, pride or greed has led us collectively to this place. When I am on patrol and encounter a rotting body in a sinkhole, I can't tell if it is a German or a Canadian or a Frenchman. It hardly seems to matter anymore. This must be the war to end all wars, the war that our children must never repeat, or it will all have been in vain.

Soldier 14: *Talbot Papineau:* *As I told you dear Beatrice, I hate this murderous business. My profession is "speeching" not fighting. I have seen so much death – and brains and blood – and marvellous human machines suddenly smashed like Humpty Dumpty… Never again shall I shoot duck again, or draw a speckled trout to gasp in my basket – I would not wish to see the death of a spider...It is over a year now since I volunteered and since then life has seemed like a ball in a game of roulette, trembling uncertain on the edge of either Beginning or End. For in effect Life will again be at the beginning if I survive. All opinions, ambitions, decisions hang suspended awaiting the verdict of chance. In the meantime, I have moments of gaiety with companions, moments of sadness when I think of home, moments of terrific anxiety and black, black moments when I question myself, my courage, and even the final success of our cause.*

(Source of italicised text of Talbot's letter is from: Gwyn, Sandra. (1992) Tapestry of War. Toronto: Harper Collins Publisher Ltd. Pg 214-215)

Soldier 15: Eleanor my dear wife, I'm near Passchendaele in Belgium. The rain has been relentless and the whole countryside is drowning in mud. The British are out fighting in it, and our turn is coming up. I've told you bits and pieces about how we've been preparing for months for yet another offensive. Well today, in our paybooks was a big stamp "KEEP YOUR MOUTHS CLOSED." I guess they are afraid we will say too much in our letters. So, I cannot tell you the Where or the When, but the HOW is only with your love. I feel strangely close to you and the children tonight. I do not know what fate has in store for me the next time I go, as they say, "over the top."

DANCE: No Man's Land Waltz: *A modern dance depicting the experience of both sides going "over the top" and fighting each other. Music can be the ominous piece that was used in between soldier rotations, or some vaguely macabre or dark instrumental piece.*

SCENE 3: *THE HOME FRONT*

The munitions workers begin their entry one line at a time, sidestepping onto the stage in a steady rhythm, with their arms making jerky movements similar to manufacturing machines. They build to a loud clanking noise, approximating a factory. Some of the workers carry singular implements like a hammer, bucket, funnel or metal object. The noise breaks sharply as the workers come forward as part of their work on the line, then pause to "read" their letters at the centre front of the stage. When each worker is finished her monologue, she turns sharply and stamps her feet to start the rhythm again.

Munitions Worker 1: Dear Gregory, you fellows have been away for two years already and finally the government is calling us women up for active duty on the home front. Till now we have been busy wrapping bandages and knitting socks and balaclava's and all that. But that's not enough anymore, not when reports keep coming back of all the casualties and the shortages on the front. Tell me Greg, brother to sister, is it really as bad as they say? Anyway, some of the girls in the neighbourhood have gone to help with the harvest. "Farmerettes" they're being called. Can you picture that! (*laughs*) Why they've even taken to wearing proper trousers and gumboots, just like the fellas. But not me, I went in for the munitions factory, making am-u-nitions!

Munitions Worker 2: *Elaine Nelson: Darling, finally I have some news that takes away the sting out of my constant worrying about you. I have a job at the Munitions factory. My first experience was when they said, "We'll arrange for you to work on the line of howitzer shells." The foreman met me at the door and he just beckoned to me. The reason why he couldn't say anything was because you couldn't have heard him! I just had to follow. I went through all these avenues and avenues of clanking, grinding, crashing machines. The foreman led me in behind one of the machines, and I stood by the wall and watched. He demonstrated how to do ONE shell, and then he stood aside and pointed to me. And so I very gingerly walked up to the machine and did what he had done. Then he stood there and said, "Again!" and I did another one. Then he just waved me goodbye and off he went. I was panic-stricken. But I got used to it.....I hope the bombs I'll be making will help to save you somehow.*

(Source of italicised text of Elaine's letter directly from oral retelling by pseudonym Elaine Nelson in: Gwyn, Sandra. (1992) Tapestry of War. Toronto: Harper Collins Publisher Ltd. Pg. 442-443)

Munitions Worker 3: Dear Wilfred, I was so relieved to hear you are in the hospital with only a simple shrapnel wound in your neck. Bad as it is, I hope it keeps you from the front lines for a while. In your letter you asked me about whether I would rather be home with the children than working the afternoon shift here. Well, of course, if you were home with us, I would. But if there is anything I could do to bring you home even a second faster, I would do it. Somehow working in this factory makes me believe I am doing just that.

Munitions Worker 4: Christopher dearest, I've been promoted to inspector! What a thrill for me to have a factory line under my supervision instead of a line of servants. The worries here are considerably more important than at the House. I am no longer concerned that the linens are crisp or the silver is polished. Instead, I lay awake at night thinking of you, worrying that I might have allowed a shell to pass that might kill one of our gunners by accident...

Munitions Worker 5: *Grace my dear friend, it's Gwen here. When you write about the special bond you and the other workers in the hospitals at the front share, I know just what you mean. Although the work here is dirty, dangerous, and even boring, this is an experience I wouldn't have missed for the world. There is a kind of spirit, an esprit de corps...My workmates are made up of everybody, every single class from high class lady to Judy O'Grady and some a few shades lower than Judy...I'm finding that they are just the same as we are, just hadn't had the chances we had for education, and it's occurred to me that we are all sisters under the skin.*

(From "Elaine Nelson" oral history, same as above.)

Munitions Worker 6: Dear Michael, at last I have some spending money of my own! Now I don't have to go to father begging and pleading when I need a new blouse or hat. It's funny, though, now that I have got a bit of ready money there isn't much to spend it on, on account of all the shortages at home. Some of my workmates are working at the factory because they want to help you boys. But some women are supporting their whole family on the wages they bring home. Its awful, but, when a soldier dies, his pay packet stops, and the family is supposed to get by on charity. About 20 of the women on my shift are widows, and they'll be more too, I suppose, before it's over. Now Michael you may not be married yet, but I know that you and Barbara write many letters to each other, so you better take care she doesn't end up a widow before she's even a bride!

Munitions Worker 7: Scott, it's happened. A terrible blast on our own shores. I was in Halifax helping out with my sister Minnie's new baby, and I seen with my own eyes what these munitions do. We could feel the earth shake when the SS Mont Blanc collided with the SS Imo in the harbour, and I went down to help in the hospital soon as I could. So many dead and still dying, so many injured. And then a major snowstorm. A few days later, Minnie and me walked down to the harbour. The whole of the city was blown down! There was nothing we could say to each other. Blocks and blocks of wrecked homes and warehouses where the week before was a crowded city. Luckily Minnie lives on the outskirts of town, or you'd be the one getting a sad telegram, not me. I handle these munitions with understanding, now.

Munitions Worker 8: *Marie:* Dear Jeremiah, Here at home we think of you constantly, and steel our hearts to the next wave of bad news. The politicians are saying they don't want people in mourning to go around wearing black any more. That's because they're afraid it would be too much for people to bear if the whole city was dressed in black. But I notice something: there is nothing that draws people together more than shared hard times. We hear the bad news and we guess at what you are sacrificing for us. It makes us roll up our sleeves and just keep going, no matter how tired or sad we are. We're keeping the home fires burning for you Jeremiah, just you believe it! As always, your sweetheart, Marie.

Curtains close.

CHOIR: *"Till the Boys Come Home (Keep the Home Fires Burning)" by Lena Guilbert Ford and Ivor Novello*

SCENE 4: *THE HOSPITAL*

The scene is the hospital. There are wounded men lying on floors, in cots, in chairs. They are bandaged in various places, or are being bandaged. One group might be playing cards. They are attended to by "blue birds," the Canadian nursing sisters, and a few doctors. In between the monologues, the tableau shows crisp movement and action.

Nurse 1: (*Walks across the stage to bring a glass of water to Grace, who has just entered on the other side.*)
Dear Father, I've hardly had a chance to catch my breath, much less a proper meal or a sleep. It's dreadful, but the wounded are arriving in droves. By the time they get to us they have already been through a long ordeal. The journey from the front is so long, and the ride so jolting that if their wounds don't kill them, the journey here might.

Grace: (*Gratefully accepts a drink of water and downs it thirstily.*)
Dear Mother, *This is my first moment to write in the past two weeks. The worst ambulance train in the world's history came in on March 24th. Cattle truck train, 350 aboard lying on stretchers and then on the floor for 38 hours. Nothing to eat or drink. No dressings. Fractures only with bandages on, splints to support broken bones nowhere to be seen. We were driving our ambulances from 7:00 to 4:30 a.m. I stopped only once for five minutes. Some very bad cases tonight. One man had most of his ear and nose off. Another had his arm off just below shoulder, and stump was hanging out. I just STEELED myself to look at them while strapping them in, and did not let myself feel sorry for them, for if I did what would happen? I drove as carefully, but as quickly as I can. A total blackout is now strictly reinforced. We are not allowed to turn on our headlights. Still, driving an ambulance means more to me than anything. I wonder if it would stir the souls of the hardened slackers back in Canada to see some of the sights over here as we see them, men in all stages of their misery and suffering, simply pouring out of trains and being taken to hospitals already packed and too full to receive them; lying on their stretchers in the reception tents, or hut floored with straw–and the most cheerful beings alive they are too. Their cheerfulness makes me brave.*

(*Source of italicised text of Grace's letter is from: Gwyn, Sandra. (1992) Tapestry of War. Toronto: Harper Collins Publisher Ltd. Pg. 453-454*)

Soldier 10: *Jeremiah:* (*Lying in a cot with shoulder bandaged.*) It finally happened Marie. I caught a "blighty" in the shoulder. When I got hit I dragged myself back to the trench, and the whole time I was crawling back there were little splashes of mud all around where the machine gun bullets were just missing me. When I finally arrived at the evacuation dugout an officer that I played with as a kid was in charge. You'll never guess: it was Michael! I was surprised to find him in the thick of battle, because he was always a fellow who liked books and such. "Michael?" I said to him, mindful of the fact that he was an officer. He didn't care about none of that. He gave me drink of cold water and cleaned up my wound a bit. He even said he'd come and visit me in the hospital if he could. Another bit of news is that I've seen other Coloured soldiers. They told me they'd joined up with the No. 2 Construction Battalion, that the government wasn't going to let them bear arms, and that most of them had been attached to the Forestry Corps. But that's changing. I'm told that because of the high number of casualties that some of our fellas are filling in spaces in the battalions, just like regular troops. I guess the government has finally figured out that White or Coloured, we all have the same red blood.

Michael enters from offstage and Grace walks over to greet him. Together they walk over to sit by Jeremiah's bedside. Stretcher bearers enter with a body on the stretcher. Doctor looks at the body and shakes his head, then goes to sit at a small desk.

Stretcher Bearer 1: Dear God, if I could write you a letter it would go something like this: When I go out into no man's land to bring back the casualties, how do I choose who is to live, and who is more likely to die because they don't get their wounds attended to in time? It happens again and again. I make my way out and I find three or four wounded fellas in a muddy shell hole. They're looking at me, and I'm looking at them, and I know – and they know – I'm only going to be able to take just one. How do I choose, dear Lord, how do I choose?

Stretcher Bearer 2: Dear Elizabeth, I don't mean to brag or nothing but I will be receiving a military medal. I feel very surprised about it, actually. I was under the impression that a hero was a soldier who was never scared, but they told me it didn't matter how I felt because it is what I did that counted. What I did was go out under fire into no man's land to bring back soldier, after soldier. To tell you the truth I couldn't help myself. I couldn't sit there any more listening to their cries while they cried out from muddy shell holes that would become their graves. All I did is what any good hearted fellow would do for his chums. If you ask me, it's the fellows I brought in who should get the medals.

Nurse 2 comes into the centre of the stage pushing Patient 1 in a wheelchair. Afterwards, she pushes him over to the group playing cards.

Nurse 2: I must tell you Louise, with all seriousness, before you make up your mind about giving your life over to nursing, you have to be prepared for it. The hours, the dedication, the willingness to do whatever is necessary. The terrible wounds and the suffering. We assist the doctors during surgery, but we are the ones who care for the boys afterwards.

And so often at night you hear them in the wards crying out for their poor mothers. It's enough to break your heart. Do you think you have what it takes, Louise? I wish you every strength in making your decision. You'll need it either way.

Nurse 3: It's your pal Lori here, grabbing a moment to write you of my dashing adventures. Usually I'm the one assisting surgeons removing shrapnel from soldiers' wounds, but last night I got a piece of my own. If you can believe it – a piece of shrapnel fell on our tent, bits of it from a dogfight going on in the sky above the hospital. We've had the occasional flyer here at the hospital. They tend to be terribly charming, and of course I'm always charming in return, because who knows how long they will live. Flying aeroplanes may be dashing, but it's oh so dangerous. In any case, you'll want to know who won. This time, it was our boy, and the German plane went down about a kilometre behind our lines. Thankfully, it didn't land on our tent!

Lieutenant Colonel Doctor John McCrae: (*sitting at a small desk*) Sirs, I am requesting more of everything – more bandages, more medicine and more nurses. As you know from my previous reports, surgical supplies are needed as much to fight infection as to close actual wounds. The bacteria which causes gas gangrene is a particularly nasty and dangerous fellow. Sometimes we need to remove three or four inches of flesh from around even a simple wound just to make sure it doesn't get infected. If we don't, our patients risk a dreadful death from even the smallest of shrapnel wounds. I trust my request will receive the attention it deserves. Sincerely, Doctor John McCrae.

Nurse 4: *Marion Landry:* Dear Madame Gagnon, I am Nursing Sister Marion Landry. I know you have already heard the sad news from Military headquarters of the passing of your precious son from wounds received at the battle of Passchendaele. I was fortunate to have tended Pierre in the week before he passed away, and I wanted you to know of the bravery he demonstrated while in our care. He was particularly cheerful and very good company with the other fellows. And he always had a kind word for us nurses. Before he passed, Pierre shared some of his favourite poetry with me – I found it very touching. He especially liked one by R.O. Bob Dorman called "The Argument." He said it was like what happened to him when he first joined up. I thought you would like to know, Madame Gagnon, that his last words were for you, his Mother. He said, "Tell Mother not to worry, and that I'll be waiting at the little house all painted red".

(*The light changes to be like a ray of light. The original three of Grace, Michael and Jeremiah walk out into that light on the centre stage, and the curtain closes behind them as they speak out the last letter.*)

Grace: Dear Mother,

Michael: Dear Father,

Jeremiah: My Dearest Sweetheart,

Together: I pray…this will be my last letter written in a time of war.

Curtains close.

CHOIR: *"In Flanders Fields" Lyrics by Lieutenant-Colonel John McCrae, several musical versions are available.*

SCENE 5: *CEREMONY OF REMEMBRANCE*

Curtains open onto the stage set with a Commonwealth War Graves Commission style headstone. The actors stand evenly spaced, two on one side and two on the other across the front of the stage. See Teacher's Guide: Ceremony of Remembrance for additional details and procedures.

Grace: On this day, November 11 in 1918, at 11 o'clock, the Armistice will be signed. Soldiers will put down their guns, and in their place find men again. The scorched earth will heal itself and become a place of green growth. For those of us involved in this struggle, healing will be slower, but hopefully it will come.

Jeremiah: We have been forged as a nation . . . people from all parts and backgrounds of Canada who gave their very best – and sometimes their all – to win this world war. Those of us who were fortunate enough to have survived carried on with a deep conviction of the importance of living a good life and in the certain knowledge of all we owe to those who gave their lives for our country.

Michael: Many of us soldiers will turn away from this war forever changed. But we do so in the hope and promise of bringing peace and development to Canada. We will go on to create many of our great national institutions. We will help shape a country where peace, order, and good government is treasured above all else.

Grace: Private Mike Pearson, who served in the Great War, became Canada's 14th Prime Minister. He went on to win a Nobel Peace Prize. He was also the father of United Nations peacekeeping. He is a shining example of a Canadian soldier who turned his back on war to do great things in the cause of World Peace and Diplomacy.

Soldier 14: *Talbot Papineau:* This war, our war, started the last century off. We called it, "The Great War." It was such a terrible war that we said it was, "the war to end all wars." Little did we know it would come to be called "World War One," with another terrible war following in our lifetime. And since then there have been too many places throughout the world where people turned to violence instead of words and compromise to solve their problems. And so, these letters help us to remember.

Jeremiah: We remember the men and women who helped make us who we are.

Grace: We remember with pride those who responded to the call of their leaders and who fought valiantly and selflessly.

Michael: We remember with affection and sadness those cut down in the promise of their youth or the richness of their middle years.

Soldier 14: *Talbot Papineau:* We remember the terrible cost of war. Let us use that knowledge to guide us towards peace.

Jeremiah: We remember with gratitude all of those Canadians who went before, whose contribution to the cause of freedom in Two World Wars, the Korean war, and several United Nations Peacekeeping and UN sanctioned NATO missions, set the course for our country.

Together: Together we remember. And we say thank you.

The Honour March takes place to music which is solemn but moving, like "Hymn to the Fallen" from the movie "Saving Private Ryan."

Once the wreathe is laid that same person asks the audience to:

"PLEASE STAND"

- **BUGLE CALL: The Last Post**

- **MOMENT OF SILENCE**

- **The moment of Silence is ended when the wreathe-layer says, "Please join us in the singing of 'O Canada'."**

- **All sing "O Canada."**

Curtains close. The performance and Ceremony of Remembrance is ended.

Scene 3: The Munitions Factory

WAITING FOR D-DAY

A Play and A Ceremony
Suitable for Performance by: Grades 4 to 8

Plot Summary:

After the choir sings *"Boogie Woogie Bugle Boy of Company B,"* **Scene 1: The Homefront** reveals street life in a busy Canadian neighbourhood which has been affected, like so many, by the war. While children's play is absorbed with aspects of war, the Russell family discuss the world situation on June 5, 1944 as Maggie and neighbour Francine prepare to work the night shift at the munitions factory. Joe, the twelve year old son of Betty and absent soldier Captain Paul, borrows his Grandpa's WWI helmet and leads the neighbourhood children in an after dinner game of "Storming Fortress Europe." He exhorts different groupings of friends to take on varied roles using a strategy that Grandpa himself says "General Eisenhower and the rest of the Allied Command should listen to." Child paratroopers drop behind enemy lines using linen napkins filched from the laundry line. An armful of toy boats is lined up to represent various types of ships in the Royal Navy convoy. The neighbourhood infantry is preparing their attack just as Mothers start calling their children in for bedtime. Joe and his mother Betty end the scene looking at the moon thinking of their loved one as Captain Paul is on the other side of the ocean (stage) looking at the moon thinking of them. The choir sings *"We'll Meet Again."*

Scene 2: On the Convoy Ship opens with General Eisenhower, General Sir Bernard Montgomery, and General Harry Crerar making the decision to commence with Operation Overlord despite the bad weather. Eisenhower relays his message to the troops. "…The hopes and prayers of liberty-loving people march with you." The soldiers tease each other about their "sea legs" and express varied motives for joining the army as well as differing attitudes about the task in front of them. Captain Paul and his assistants on deck talk about the immense resources gathered to begin the fight and then give a pep talk to the soldiers. The soldiers are emboldened and ready to go, leaving the performance space by storming down the centre isle and through the audience.

Scene 3: The Dance of Juno Beach is a modern dance symbolizing the battle with its three groupings of support: Air Force, Navy, and Infantry.

Scene 4: The Invasion Has Begun returns to the home front, where Joe returns from his morning newspaper run with the exciting news that the Invasion has finally successfully started. The family gathers around the paper to read the first hand reports which are based on actual newspaper articles. They are united in their hope that this is the beginning of the end. The choir sings *"Let There Be Peace On Earth"* by Jill Jackson and Sy Miller.

Scene 5: The Ceremony of Remembrance is led by Joe, General Crerar, Betty, and Soldier Pat. The Cast and Crew enter the stage during the Honour March to solemn but moving music like *"Hymn to the Fallen"'* from the movie *"Saving Private Ryan."* The laying of the wreathe is followed by the *Last Post* and the *Moment of Silence*, which ends with the singing of *"O Canada."*

Acting Roles:

Speaking roles: 25 individual roles
- 6 groups of singing or game playing children (flexible numbers)

Group scenes for additional non-speaking roles:
- neighbourhood mothers
- children playing
- soldiers on ship waiting to disembark

Music / Choral Options:

"Boogie Woogie Bugle Boy of Company B" by the Andrews Sisters

"We'll Meet Again" by Vera Lynn

"Let There Be Peace on Earth" by Jill Jackson and Sy Miller

Dance Options:

Dance of Juno Beach: A modern jazz dance symbolizing the battle with it's three groupings of support from the Air Force, Navy, and Infantry.

[Previous Performances: Rockcliffe Park Public School, Ottawa, Ontario. Directed by Barbara Brockmann 2004, 2007]

CHARACTERS AND COSTUMES

In order of appearance. Roles with full names are based on real people.
Use the character list below to record the names of your cast members!

Joe: (*an eleven year old boy, shorts, plaid shirt, sneakers*) _____

Except for Joe, all other children's roles can be filled by boys or girls. The boys' group can include tomboys. All children should be dressed in appropriate 1940's fashions. Fairly neat shirts, shorts, skirts, ankle socks, sneakers or open toed sandals. Avoid modern styles like t-shirts with brand symbols or neon colours. Hair may be done up in pig tails, braids or pony tails.

Kid 1: _____
Max: _____
French Singing Group: _____
_____
Hand Clapping Group: _____
_____

ISBN: 9781554950683

"Jeux des mains" Group: _____
_____

Skipping Group: _____
_____

Ball Group: _____
_____

Boys Group: _____
_____

Grand-maman: *(nice dress, nylons and shoes, pearls, knitting)* _____
Grandpa: *(vest, slacks, white shirt with bowtie, newspaper and pipe)* _____
Betty: *(motherly, middle class working clothes, apron)* _____
Maggie: *(dressed in conservative suit, carrying overalls)* _____
Francine: *(dressed as "Rosie the Riveter" with hair tied up in red scarf, overalls, lunchpail, workboots)* _____

Kid 2: _____
Kid 3: _____
Kid 4: _____

Soldier 1: _____
Soldier 2: _____

General Dwight D. Eisenhower: *(cap, American general uniform)* _____
General Harry Crerar: *(red beret, Canadian general uniform)* _____
General Sir Bernard Montgomery: *(beret, British general uniform)* _____

Captain Paul: _____
Soldier 3: _____
Soldier 4: _____

Davey: *(young soldier, seasick)* _____
George: *(crusty)* _____
Pat: *(Newfoundlander, good spirited)* _____

Johnny: *(worried)* _____
Rusty: *(gambler, lively)* _____
Al: *(serious)* _____

"Dance of Juno Beach" Group:

In black, barefoot, with additions which respond to the branch of the military they represent:
- paratroopers – large white translucent squares
- navy – a navy collar of blue edged with a white stripe
- infantry – strips of camouflage fabric tied around their heads and upper arms or wrists

Scene Four: The Invasion Has Begun

SCENE 1: *THE HOMEFRONT*

CHOIR: *"Boogie Woogie Bugle Boy of Company B"* by the Andrews Sisters

Curtains remain drawn. Joe ambles out across the apron of the stage with a heavy newspaper bag over his shoulder. At centre stage he pulls out a newspaper and reads the front page.

Joe: (*slowly, deliberately*) June 5, 1944. Headline: Fighting continues in the Pacific, African, and European arenas of war. Slow but steady advancement in the Pacific, in Africa, in Italy. (*sighs and starts to make up headline*) Nazi's still in control of the rest of Fortress Europa. More dads and moms are called to join Army, Navy, Air Force. Everything is the same. Nothing is the same. Ha!

Kid 1: (*Running on to stage*) Joe! The enemy is on their way. We need more reinforcements.

Joe: I'm with you! I have to finish my paper route.

Kid 1: Join us when we try to take Dieppe again!

Curtains open fully to reveal a front porch tableau: Grandpa in rocking chair with pipe and newspaper, Grandmama is knitting socks, and mother Betty is ironing a large stack of linen napkins and pillow cases. Children enter the performance area from various directions, laughing and playing. When they reach their "positions," they freeze into tableau. The Singing Group enters from the back, holding hands in pairs and skipping.

Singers and Max: (*same tune as French folk-song, "Napoléon avait cinq cents soldats"*)

> Les Canadiens avaient cinq cents soldats,
> Les Canadiens avaient cinq cents soldats,
> Les Canadiens avaient cinq cents soldats,
> Marchant d'un même pas !

(When the singing group reaches the front they are interrupted by Francine who has stepped out onto the stage and is looking for Max (Maxime or Maxine, depending on the actor/actress)

Francine: Maxine? Maxine! Viens. Préparons-nous pour ce soir.

Maxine: D'accord Maman. Je m'en viens. (*Bids goodbye to friends and skips off stage. The friends form into their respective groups and freeze in a tableau until their time to perform. Then they freeze again until the Boys Group activates them.*)

Hand Clapping Group: (*in pairs*)
> I know a man named Hitler,
> He was very bad
> He got into power
> And he made the world so sad, sad, sad.

Emperor Hirohito,
He lives in Japan,
He wants the South Pacific
To be his own Sampan, pan pan.

They send out their soldiers
To take over the land,
So we have to send our Dads
To fight back all we can, can, can.

Hello operator,
Give me number four,
They'll be another year of war, war, war.

"Jeux des mains" Group: (*In a circle, with a more elaborate hand clapping choreography*)
Un, deux, trois, quatre,
Mon char d'assault
A mal aux pattes
Tirez- le, par la queue
Il ira, bien mieux,
Dans un jour ou deux.

Skipping Group: (*line up waiting to skip at a long rope*)
Not last night
But the night before
Ninety-nine soldiers knocked at my door.
They said,
"ewwww, ahhhhhhhh
What side are you on?
I said, "The Allies have the power
SO YOU BE GONE!

Ball Group: (*bouncing or throwing balls to a counter-rhythm*)
A-Day, B-Day, here comes C-Day,
We want D-Day,
D-Day, DECISION DAY!

(*Boys tiptoe out on stage like they are sneaking up on the girls, and then launch into their piece energetically.*)

Boys:
Whistle while you work,
Hitler is a jerk,
Mussolini is a meanie
Now the world's berserk!
(*pause*)
JUST LIKE YOU!

(*Girls pretend to be outraged and run after the boys off the performance area.*)

Grand-maman: (*knitting socks*) Finally we get some peace and quiet. It can't be much louder than if we were on the battlefield ourselves.

Grandpa: (*lowering newspaper and taking pipe out of mouth*) I'd say that Vimy and Passchendaele were a good bit louder than this, my dear.

Joe: (*rushing in*) Grandpa, Grandpa, can I use your Great War helmet? We're planning an invasion and I need to be protected.

Betty: (*exasperated*) Joe, how many times do I have to tell you? You know that isn't a toy! You know that helmet saved Grandpa's life many times in the Great War and it's a family treasure.

Grandpa: Why do you need it boy?

Joe: (*very animated*) Grandpa, me and the others are planning to breech Fortress Europa. We're parachuting behind the lines of the Atlantic Wall and we're going to attack from behind. Then the rest of the Allied forces will surprise the enemy by attacking from the ocean side.

Grandpa: Hmmmm, that's quite a good plan you have got there Joe. General Eisenhower and the rest of the Allied command should listen to you. In the circumstances it's clear you'll need my helmet. Sure, go and get it.

Joe: Thanks Grandpa, you're the best!

Grand-maman: Its seems like war is the only game the children are playing these days. (*Shakes head in despair.*) But I guess I can understand that ... five years of fighting so far and it just seems to get worse. First it was just Europe, then Eastern Europe, then Turkey, then Africa, then the South Pacific, and Hong Kong and China.

Grandpa: Actually dear, China was first, when that no good Japanese Emperor Hirohito invaded. Then Hitler bombed Guernica to help out that Spanish scoundrel Franco. When those things happened we knew it was only a matter of time until the whole world was at war.

Grand-maman: And now it seems that anyone with two legs is in uniform. We've got neighbours in the army, the navy, the air force and the merchant marine. Even the girls are working in war factories. To tell you the truth, if I wasn't looking for news of our Paul and the other boys from our neighborhood, I couldn't bear to listen to the radio or read the newspapers..

Betty: (*As grandparents are speaking she pulls out a worn envelope from her apron, and lovingly, longingly fingers it.*) I…..I know what you mean.

(*Young woman in a suit rushes into room.*)

Maggie: Betty, help me get my seam straight? (*Hands Betty a pencil, and stands on a chair. Betty draws a line down the back of Maggie's legs.*) Bonjour Maman, Hello Dad.

Grandma: Bonjour. Are there still no nylons in the store these days?

Maggie: No, Grand-maman. All the nylon and plastics are needed for the war effort. There are none left for fashion!

Grand-maman: Why aren't you wearing your factory uniform dear?

Maggie: I have my interview tonight. I know the bosses are pleased with my work as a safety inspector on the factory line, but I want to look older and more serious to get this job. We sure could use the extra money. So Grandpa, what's in the news tonight?

Grandpa: Same old, same old. Rationing of food and supplies everywhere, bombs in England, submarines in the Atlantic and Pacific, planes in the sky. All of them dropping bombs on the Germans, Japanese, and their friends, but none of it seems to get us anywhere.

(*Francine walks into scene with Max carrying his/her pillow. She is dressed like "Rosie the Riveter" in overalls with her hair tied up, and is carrying a lunch pail.*)

Francine: Bonjour les amis. Comment ça-va ce-soir?

Grand-maman: Bonjour Francine. Ça-va assez bien mais on n'a pas eu de nouvelles. Pas bien, pas mal.

Betty: (*takes the pillow from Max and smiles*) Let me take the pillow from you Max. It's always a pleasure to have you stay for a sleepover. You go and join the kids. They're out back saving democracy. (*chuckles*)

Max: Thanks Mrs. Russell! I'll go and help them! I'm going to try to get my dad out of the prisoner of war camp again.

Grandpa: Wait a second Max. (*pulls a bag of candies out of his pocket*) Why don't you bring this bag of candies to the soldiers, sailors and paratroopers out back. And don't forget to give some to the Merchant Marine and the Medical Corps!

Max: Thanks Mr. Russell!

Grandpa: (*waits for Max to leave*) How is Max doing now?

Francine: He still wakes up crying, but the nightmares aren't so bad. My mother keeps her hope alive by praying that Jacques is in a prisoner of war camp, but I keep my hope alive by working in the munitions factory. It's so crazy. I fill the bombs with explosives and pray they will somehow bring the war to an end a little faster. But I also pray the bombs don't land on innocent families who are anxious for their soldier husbands to come home, just like us.

Maggie: Goodness knows we all feel the same.

Francine: On y va! Merci Betty for looking after Max again while I work the night shift. Here, I've brought you my ration of eggs to thank you. (*Opens lunch bucket and hands over two eggs.*)

Betty: Thanks Francine. Hopefully I can use them for a victory cake sometime soon!

(*Maggie and Francine exit. Grand-maman takes the eggs from Betty and kisses each one. Gingerly leaves, holding the eggs up carefully. Grandpa folds the newspaper, picks up chair and heads offstage. Betty leaves laundry behind as she carries other chair offstage. Children enter performance area from all directions. Joe takes milk crate from under the laundry basket and puts it in centre. Stands on it.*)

Joe: Okay - you bomber pilots from the Royal Canadian Air Force have already done your work softening up the enemy. (*kids nod in agreement*) Now we are going to be paratroopers from the 1st Canadian Parachute Battalion.

Kid 1: We'll be the first soldiers of the entire invasion force to experience the day of decision!

Joe: Yeah! Once you land behind enemy lines, your first mission is to assemble your unit. You have to blow up those big German guns along the shoreline and destroy bridges used by the Panzer units during a counterattack. You have to accomplish your mission before bedtime, oops, I mean daybreak. Here are your parachutes. (*Grabs the newly ironed items from the laundry pile and hands them out.*)

Kid 2: Wait! Who is going to guard the home front? We have to do a countdown.

Joe: Eeny, meeny, miney moe, catch an enemy by the toe, when he hollers don't let him go, eeny meeny, minney moe. Okay, YOU (*Max*) have to guard the home front. For everyone else, it's Decision Day! Let's call it D-Day!

(*Kids scatter, except for Max who is clearly unhappy, but resigned, about being left. As kids scatter, Betty comes to collect laundry basket. Notices the items are gone.*)

Max: Une, deux, trois...(*is interrupted*)

Betty: Joe? Joe! Did you take my ironed laundry AGAIN?

(*Max smiles sweetly and says nothing. Continues counting once Betty leaves frustrated.*)

Max: ... quatre, cinq, six, sept, huit, neuf, dix...Pret ou non, je viens!

(*During the counting, Kid 3 comes rushing in with an armful of toy boats and collides with Max just as she finishes. They pick them up together.*)

Kid 3: Hey, you almost sunk my destroyer!

Max: Your destroyer?

Kid 3: Well, I think it's a destroyer. But really, I can't decide if these should be convoy ships, freighters, destroyers, frigates, corvettes or minesweepers. I guess us guys in the Royal Canadian Navy are going to need all of them. Let me see ... (*lifts them one by one and places them carefully in front*).

Max: Start with the minesweeper to clear the way! (*places the biggest one in the front*)

Kid 3: These two can be the assault ships HMCS Algonquin and HMCS Sioux, to bombard enemy installations.

Max: Then you'll need convoy ships to bring in the troops. (*They organize the last few ships and stand up satisfied.*)

Together: Done!

(*Paratroopers have been sneaking silently back on stage. Joe is among them.*)

Joe: Mission accomplished! Now we're ready for the landing craft to open, and for the infantry to make their attack. Is the medical core standing by? (*Child comes running on stage with a play medical bag and a Red Cross insignia around her arm.*)

Kid 4: Check!

Joe: This is the moment we've been waiting for, training for. (*hands out sticks for weapons*) Whether you're on the home front, in the air, on the sea, or on the ground, we're in this together. Soldiers, prepare to disembark!

Shouting from all corners of backstage: Joe! Katie! Ella! Simon! Avya! Max! (*Children look guiltily around and start to tiptoe off in all directions.*) Time to come in...It's bed time...**NOW!**

(*Kids wave goodbye to each other, and resignedly walk off stage. Joe wanders to one side to look up at the "moon." Betty comes out looking for Joe. He hands her his collection of now soiled laundry items and she shakes her head but takes them. Then she notices he is sad.*)

Betty: A penny for your thoughts, son.

Joe: I was thinking about Dad. And what he might be doing tonight. He's been over in England for two years Mom. He joined up right after we lost Dieppe. He's been training and training and training. When are they ever going to attack, so we can win and he can come home?

Betty: I think they must be getting ready soon Joe. (*Pulls envelope out of her pocket.*) Paul's last letter to us didn't say much. That's a sure sign the censors are telling the men to give no clues about what the plans are, in case the letter falls into enemy hands. Your Dad wants to come home you know. And he will come home, God willing, as soon as the job of kicking Hitler and the Nazi's out of Europe is done.

Joe: I sure wish it was soon.

Betty: So do I darling. Now, let's enjoy the moon. Maybe he's on the other side of the Atlantic, looking at the same moon, thinking about us.

(Paul steps out on the other side of the stage. He is dressed in full army gear, ready for battle, and is looking at the "moon", holding a letter against his heart.)

CHOIR: *"We'll Meet Again"* by Vera Lynn

(After the song the two parties slip behind the curtains.)

SCENE 2: *ON THE CONVOY SHIP*

(Curtains are closed. Two soldiers are standing centre stage in front of curtains, holding clipboards and conversing in low tones)

Soldier 1: Let me tell you Willy - something BIG has gotta be coming down. I heard that General Eisenhower, the Supreme Allied Commander, has just arrived to meet with General Bernard Montgomery who is the commander of all land forces in Europe.

Soldier 2: Hey, isn't that General Harry Crerar? He's our big boss – the Canadian general in command of all Canadian troops in Northern Europe!

Soldier 1: Oh, oh. Here they all come. I think we better skedaddle! (*exit stage left*)

(General Dwight D. "Ike" Eisenhower (Supreme Allied Commander) walks out from stage right and across the front of the closed curtains with General Harry Crerar (Commander of the Canadian troops) and General Sir Bernard "Monty" Montgomery (Commander-in-Chief of the Invasion)

Eisenhower: Harry and Monty, the weather reports are just in. It's not exactly the weather we were hoping for, but I believe that we should launch Operation Overlord tonight. What do you think Generals?

Crerar: I agree with you Ike. The men are aboard the ships, and the forecast says the bad weather will lift for only about twenty four hours. If we don't go tonight we'll have to wait another two weeks. It's taken two years to get to this point and I say we're right and ready.

Montgomery: Ike, Harry's correct. We've got hundreds of thousands of our forces primed and already on their way. I say let the invasion begin!

Crerar: The liberation of Europe is a heavy weight to bear Gentlemen, but the soldiers, seamen, and air force crews already out there on or over the Channel tonight are willing to bear the brunt of it.

Montgomery: As this promises to be a defining moment in the history of western civilization I believe that the men deserve a few words. As the Supreme Allied commander, Ike, why don't you give it to them?

Eisenhower: Most appropriate, Monty. And it so happens I have come prepared. (*Steps forward as the other two stand a kind of proud guard on each side of him and delivers his message with great energy.*)

Soldiers, sailors, and airmen of the Allied Expeditionary Forces, you are about to embark upon a great crusade, toward which we have striven these many months. The eyes of the world are upon you. The hopes and prayers of liberty-loving people everywhere march with you.

(*The Generals turn to each other and firmly shake hands. Walk offstage with determination.*)
(*Curtains open and the soldiers are sitting on stage as they would in the hold of a convoy ship. Some are playing cards, others writing letters. Paul stands apart and holds a letter from his wife Betty which he is reading and treasuring.*)

Soldier 3: Excuse me sir, I'm sorry to interrupt, are you reading the Orders of the Day from Allied Command?

Captain Paul: Uhh, no. (*a bit embarrassed*) Actually, it's a letter from my wife Betty, and my son Joe.

Soldier 3: I understand sir. I've been thinking about my family too.

Captain Paul: I suppose it's only natural in the circumstances. My young son just got a job delivering newspapers. And he wants to donate his earnings to the war effort.

Soldier 3: You must be proud of him sir.

Captain Paul: I am. And when he learns of what is happening here tonight he'll be proud of us.

(*Freeze. Tableau switch.*)

Davey: Ohhhhh….. Uppppppp….. Dowwwnnn. This boat ride is killing me.

Pat: Davey doesn't have his sea legs.

George: His sea legs? You need gills to get through this chop.

Pat: Sure this is nothing boys! Back home in Newfoundland we'd be skittling and dancing in a breeze as fresh as this. Nothing to worry about lads. And Davey, this is a ship, a boat is what we use for fishing.

Davey: Oh mannn….. boat or a ship, I think I'm dying. When I was a kid I couldn't even face rafting on the Saugeen River.

George: When you were a kid? You're still a kid. Aren't you only eighteen?

Davey: Seventeen. Ohhhhhhhhhh…….. My brother was killed at Dieppe. And there was nothing going to stop me from enlisting. Just don't let anyone know I'm underage.

Pat: I'll tell you lads, this is good weather for an assault. It's night and the seas are a bit roughish. So we've got the element of surprise on our side. The Jerries will never expect us.

George: Hey Pat. You're from Newfoundland. You're not even a Canadian. What the heck are you doing here?

Pat: Like Davey, I got a good reason. Back in the First War, my grandfather was killed fighting at the Somme. It was July 1st, 1916 - the blackest day in the history of Newfoundland. So now they're at it again and I'll be darned if I won't do my part – even if I have to join up with you Canucks to do it!

(*Freeze. Soldier 4 walks briskly across the backstage.*)

Captain Paul: These boys are from families across Canada. From farms and from factories. From the Okanagan Valley to the Gaspe. They could have stayed at home and worked hard to provide Canada and our allies with the food and supplies needed to fight this war. But these men chose different. They chose to be part of history.

Soldier 4: Sir, I was just up on deck and it's incredible out there! You should see it! You should hear it Sir! The sky is filled with fighters and bombers. There's thousands of them up there. What a noise! And the ships! Holy Crumbles! (*he looks at paper*) Reports say there are more than 5,000 convoy vessels with us tonight. And! there's 700 warships and six battleships. There are more than 150,000 men heading for the beaches of Northern France with us at this very moment. This is it Sir! This is it!

Captain Paul: Thank you. The word is out! We've got our orders from General Crerar. It's time to inform the men.

(*Freeze*)

Rusty: Alright, who's up for a hand of cards? Come on Johnny, just a quick game. Or maybe a few! What about you Al?

Al: For crying out loud! A hand of cards? What is it with you Rusty?

Johnny: Yeah. Like we have nothing else to worry about 'cept about owing you money. Put 'em away Rusty. There ain't none of us wants to play cards. Not tonight anyway.

(*Freeze. Captain Paul and Soldier 3 enter.*)

Soldier 3: Attention!

(*The men stand up and fall to attention in a line facing him across the front of the stage.*)

Captain Paul: At ease, at ease. (*Soldiers stand at ease.*) Well, gentlemen, the moment is upon us. We have waited for this night for five years. Welcome to Operation Overlord. It is my proud duty to tell you that you're part of the biggest invasion in the history of the world. There are over 150,000 soldiers just like you green faced devils waiting to land on the beaches of Normandy at dawn's light.

Soldier 3: Reports tell us that allied forces have already dropped thousands of paratroopers behind enemy lines and bomber planes are doing their best to keep the enemy busy while we come at them from the front.

Captain Paul: The battle for Fortress Europa has begun. This is what we've been training for men, and I needn't tell you that the whole world is watching us tonight. Do your duty and give it your best. And remember your families back home and that their prayers and wishes go with you.

Soldier 3: We are landing at Juno Beach. Remember that name Gentlemen, Juno Beach.

Captain Paul: At Juno we will establish a beachhead. Our immediate objective is to capture three small seaside towns. From there we will advance ten miles inland. Rest assured your efforts today and over the next few weeks and months will mark your place in one of Canada's finest moments. God be with you and take care.

(*Paul exits. The men relax and turn to talk to each other.*)

Pat: Well, sure we knew we was going to be landing on a beach. What else did they have in mind?

Al: Not just a beach, Pat. That French beach is our foothold on the continent.

George: So we take Juno Beach, then what?

Soldier 3: Then we keep going, and going, and going, till them Nazi's are done. That's what it's all about boys. And by God we'll do it!

Davey: Going, and going, and going. Ohhhhhhhhh.......I'm already gone!

Paul's Voice offstage: All men stand to. All men stand to. Prepare to disembark.

Soldier 3: This is it fellas. Our chance to free Europe. When that ramp goes down get ready to move ... and I mean fast.

(*Soldiers move quickly into a double line behind Pat and Ralph facing the audience. Ominous music. Count to three and then jump over the edge of the stage, charging down the centre of the auditorium/gym keeping body low, guns pointed up, and looking all around. Exit from back of auditorium/gym)*

SCENE THREE: *THE DANCE OF JUNO BEACH*

Dance indicating the commencement of "Operation Overlord". Musical possibilities have included appropriate selections from the movie soundtrack "*Master and Commander*" and "*Titanic.*"

Dancers wear black with props which indicate the branch of the military they are representing. The dance illustrates three aspects of the invasion:

- from the air (paratroopers): *dancers swirl with large translucent white squares*
- the navy: *dancers miming the handling and pulling of a large rope*
- the infantry: *dancers crawling, climbing, rolling across the stage in active battle*

The dance should end with all three groups on stage, striving together.

SCENE FOUR: *THE INVASION HAS BEGUN*

Scene opens on the empty neighbourhood stage. Joe rushes in wearing his newspaper bag waving a newspaper.

Joe: Mom! Grandpa! Grand-maman! Come quick! It's here!

Betty: What's here? Is there a telegram? Is it about your father?

Joe: No, no telegram. Look Mom, look! Look Grandpa! Look Grand-maman! It's started, the invasion has started.

Grandpa: Well I'll be! He's right. The boy is right. The invasion started last night. Just about the same time you kids were outside playing.

Joe: Woo Hoo! Fortress Europa isn't a fortress anymore.

(*Francine and Maggie return from work. Max and Grand-maman walk out wearing an apron and drying hands with a dishcloth. Francine and Max embrace.*)

Grand-maman: Qu'est-ce qui c'est passé?

Grandpa: (*getting teary eyed*) It's finally happened, ma belle! Here, you read it daughter-in-law. My eyes are getting uh…itchy.

Betty: On the night of the invasion, paratroopers landed behind enemy lines. They destroyed bridges and gun batteries in advance of the main occupying force. Despite rough seas and heavy winds the Armada of ships carrying more than 150,000 men landed their precious cargo on the shores of Europe.

Max and Joe: (*high fiving*) Holy Mackerel! That's just like we played it!

Francine: Look, page three has a letter from a Canadian Captain. Isn't that Paul's rank?

Betty: Now I can't read it. Here Joe, you try.

Joe: Letter from France. Captain tells wife His Battalion has Fared Well In Two Scraps. By Ralph Allen.

This is a Soldiers letter from France. It is the letter of one soldier written to one family. With a little imagination we can see that this letter could be the letter of any soldier to any family in Great Britain, Canada or the United States.

The letter was dictated to me just one hour ago by a 37 year old Captain in a Canadian Assault Battalion in the near reaches of Juno Beach on Tuesday morning. The Captain's wife may find the letter a little less romantic than she's used to, but the Captain knew that I would cable the letter for publication in newspapers across Canada.

Dearest Betty, ...Hey Mom! That must be you! (*Passes it to Maggie*)

Maggie: I am so glad I have this way of telling you so soon that I am well.

You probably know more of the details of the invasion than I do from your reading of the newspapers and listening to the radio. All I can tell you is what I've seen and how I feel. Before we hit the beaches, the sea was full of ships and boats of every kind and size. The big ships were packed full of troops, tanks, vehicles, and supplies. To see it you'd have thought an entire city was moving across the Channel. And the sky was full of bombers and fighter planes. And then they started shelling the beaches. What a racket!

(*Passes it to Francine.*)

Francine: I'd be telling you a lie if I said I wasn't scared. Only a fool wouldn't be scared. But I was steady and I was calm and knew what I had to do. The thought of you and our children kept me going.

Our battalion has already fought two hard battles and so far we've done alright. The worst was landing on the beaches. Despite heavy shelling the Germans were well dug in behind barbed wire and huge concrete bunkers. But we cleared them out and just kept going.

There is one thing I hardly know how to say. Some of our friends and neighbours will probably start receiving telegrams telling them that their sons or husbands have been killed or wounded.

(*Passes it.*)

Grand-maman: There is not much I can say about this except that before we landed many of the men steadied themselves with prayer. All of them were brave in the face of the enemy knowing we had to get the job done. And that's what it's about:

Getting the Job Done. This is just the beginning, I know. But it's the beginning of the end of the War.

You know my love is always with you, Betty. Please give a big hug to Joe, Dad, Maman, and my sister Maggie. Give my best to the neighbours, especially Francine and Max. I send you a kiss. Someday soon I will give it to you myself, All my love, Paul.

Francine: My goodness what a letter! The Captain's right. This is only the beginning of the end of the war. That means there's still lots more for everyone to do.

Betty: We all have to keep doing our bit.

Grand-maman: Keep knitting socks for the soldiers.

Maggie: Keep working in the factories and on the farms.

Grandpa: Keep being frugal.

Joe and Max: Keep the home fires burning.

Betty: While it isn't the end of war, it is the beginning of peace, and that's something else we can do, make sure that peace begins with each of us.

(*Curtains close.*)

CHOIR: "*Let There Be Peace On Earth*" by Sy Miller and Jill Jackson

SCENE 5: *THE CEREMONY OF REMEMBRANCE*

Curtains open onto the stage set with a Commonwealth War Graves Commission style headstone. The actors stand evenly spaced, two on one side and two on the other across the front of the stage. **See Teacher's Guide:** *Ceremony of Remembrance for additional details and procedures.*

Joe: D-Day WAS the beginning of the end. In Normandy, the Canadians who landed on the beaches still faced enormous difficulties. But they stuck to the job with their British and American buddies, and got the job done. By May, of 1945, the peace in Europe was won.

Betty: Almost one in ten Canadians wore a uniform during the war. Of that number over 100,000 were killed, wounded or captured. Despite the enormous sacrifices none of this stopped the soldiers or their families from giving the war effort their all. We are not a country that starts wars, but if someone starts a just fight, we'll be there to help to sort it out.

General Crerar: How did Canada change from 1939 to 1945? We changed from being mostly a farming country into one that could look after most of its needs. We became a country that was able to equip, train, and man the world's 3rd largest navy, its 5th largest air force, and an army that could fight on two major fronts at the same time.

Soldier Pat: It's like Canada became a new country. A country that was able to set off in new directions, with a new purpose. Like building a society that looks after its citizens, and then opened its doors to millions of immigrants and refugees. We started out small and inward looking, and ended up as one of the world's most international of nations.

Betty: And so, today we remember the men and women who helped make us who we are.

Soldier Pat: We remember with pride those who fought bravely and selflessly.

Joe: We remember with affection and sadness those cut down in the promise of their youth or the richness of middle age.

Betty: We remember the terrible cost of war. Let us use that knowledge to guide us towards peace.

General Crerar: We remember with gratitude all of those Canadians who went before, whose contribution to the cause of freedom through Two World Wars, the Korean war, several United Nations Peacekeeping missions, and UN sanctioned NATO missions, forged a positive direction for our country and for the world today.

Together: Together we remember. And we thank you.

The Honour March takes place to music which is solemn but moving, like "Hymn to the Fallen" from the movie "Saving Private Ryan."

Once the wreathe is laid that same person asks the audience to:

"PLEASE STAND"

- **BUGLE CALL**: The Last Post

- **MOMENT OF SILENCE**

- **The moment of Silence is ended when the wreathe-layer says, "Please join us in the singing of 'O Canada'."**

- **All sing "O Canada."**

Curtains close. The performance and Ceremony of Remembrance is ended.

Scene Two: On the Convoy Ship

REMEMBERING KOREA, 1950 to 1953

A Play and A Ceremony

Suitable for Performance By: Grades 6 and up

Plot Summary:

Tony and his gang of friends, Mathieu, Vern, Digger, and brothers Charlie and Brian are having an end-of summer high school reunion picnic in **Scene 1: The News** before they head off to jobs or further schooling. Their future directions seem clear. The party is interrupted by an important CBC radio broadcast by Prime Minister St. Laurent urging all able bodied men to join the Korean War effort. The whole gang decides to sign up together for a variety of different reasons, much to the anguish of Tony's mother and younger sister Katie, and the pride of their girlfriends Irene and Susan.

In **Scene 2: Recruitment Centre** Colonel Jim Stone and his cohort discuss whether this "action" will be more like the disaster of Hong Kong in '41 or the success of Italy in the late 40's. In either case, Col. Stone resolves that the soldiers will get the training they need. The choir hints at the distance between families with the song *"Goodnight Irene."* The gang of new soldiers and their friends hold a **Scene 3: Jive Goodbye Dance Party**.

Once in **Scene 4: Korea** the soldiers are greeted by the strange but true sight of a choir singing *"If I'd known You Were Coming I'd Have Baked a Cake."* They are surprised by the "Land of the Morning Calm" which appears both less calm and more mountainous than expected. Bill Boss, a Canadian war correspondent, covers the story of the Battle of Kap'yong (*Gapyeong*), where this group of young soldiers figures prominently. As a counterpoint to the awarding of the US Presidential Distinguished Unit Citation for their efforts in this crucial battle to save Seoul we learn that Charlie is likely dead.

In **Scene 5: Seoul** Bill Boss then meets up with a youthful Pierre Berton who is interviewing Red Cross worker Muriel White. Berton also interviews Mrs. Tak, a Korean refugee, with the assistance of translator Dickie and Tony who are momentarily on re-assigned duties from the front.

During **Scene 6: Night Patrol** the Chinese propaganda machine broadcasts its message across the valley as the soldiers take a break. They dream out loud of home and peace. Later, it becomes clear that Digger, who has just decided to ask Susan to be his "girl" and who is on his last night patrol, has been killed. Throughout, Katie's monologues about what she reads or doesn't read in the newspaper provide a counterpoint to how the Korean War is fading from view at home.

When the remaining friends finally reach **Scene 7: Homecoming**, no crowd greets them except the family and loyal girlfriends. Susan collapses when she hears the news that Digger has been killed just before the Armistice. Despite their sorrow the group confirms what their sacrifice meant to the democratic "free world" and the South Korean people. The choir sings *"Let There Be Peace on Earth."*

ISBN: 9781554950683

The play is followed by **Scene 8: Ceremony of Remembrance**, which includes a reflection on what the Korean and other wars of Canadian involvement have meant to us. All the Cast and Crew enter the stage during the Honour March to solemn but moving music. The laying of the wreathe is followed by the Last Post and the Moment of Silence, which ends with the singing of *"O Canada."*

Acting Roles:

Speaking Roles: 22 individual roles, 3 voice-over roles

Group scenes for additional non-speaking roles:
- Opening scene picnic
- Jive Goodbye Dance Party
- Korean refugees, merchants, and wounded soldiers in a marketplace

Music / Choral Options:

- **Percussion:** military drum beat
- **Choir:** *"Goodnight Irene"* by Huddie "Led Belly" Ledbetter
- **Soundtrack:** *Street Scene*
- **Choir:** *"If I'd known You Were Coming I'd Have Baked a Cake"* by Eileen Barton
- **Interlude:** *Traditional Korean music*
- **Percussion:** wind and air sounds
- **Choir:** *"Let There be Peace on Earth"* by Jill Jackson and Sy Miller.
- **Honour March:** *"Hymn to the Fallen"* from the movie *"Saving Private Ryan"*

Dance Options:

Jive Goodbye Dance Party to *"Swing the Mood"* by Glen Miller. Boys in uniform and girls in party dresses dance together before the boys leave for Korea.

[Previous performances: Fisher Park Public and Summit Alternative Public School, Ottawa Ontario.]
[Directed by Barbara Brockmann (2002) and Dale Hayward (2005 and 2007)]

CHARACTERS AND COSTUMES

In order of appearance. Roles with full names are based on real people.
Use the character list below to record the names of your cast members!

The young men and women have just graduated from high school.

Tony: *(good natured, intelligent, loyal)* _____

Mathieu: *(scholarly, patient)* _____

Vern: *(strong sense of justice, forceful, frustrated)* _____

Digger: *(a self-described party guy and babe magnet)* _____

Brian: *(brother to Charlie, lively)* _____

Charlie: *(younger brother, pleasant)* _____

Clothing for <u>Scene 1</u> is summer 1950's outfits: white t-shirts or plaid shirts with short sleeves rolled up, sneakers, baggy pants or shorts. Clothing for <u>Scene 3</u> and the rest are WWII uniforms.

Katie: *(pre-teen tomboy in overalls and messy pigtails at the start of the play; evolves to a more mature teenager)* _____

Mom: *(1950's dress which can be dressed down with an apron, or dressed up with a sweater and pearls for later scenes)* _____

Susan: *(Digger's girlfriend; slightly glamorous and "dishy"; Outfit for opening picnic, fancy dress for jive party; conservative outfit for homecoming)* _____

Irene: *(Tony's girlfriend; intelligent, attractive, loyal. Outfit for opening picnic, fancy dress for jive party; conservative outfit for homecoming)* _____

Radio Announcer: *(voice over only)* _____

Prime Minister Louis St. Laurent: *(voice over only)* _____

(Both officers dress in army gear.)

Colonel Jim Stone: *(frustrated, realistic)* _____

Officer 1: *(enthusiastic, naive)* _____

Jive Dance group at the party: *(Party clothes from the 1950's)* _____

Sheila, Lisa and Heather: *(girlfriends at the dance)* _____

DJ photographer: _____

Bill Boss: *(leather jacket, glasses, wool pants, beret, paisley scarf)* _____

Pierre Berton: *(wool army outfit, trench coat over that, beret, moustache, carrying old style camera)* _____

Muriel White: (*army pants, white t-shirt, lab coat, red cross band on arm*) _____

Dickie: (*middle aged South Korean soldier, dressed in army uniform*) _____

Mrs. Tak and Sister: (*middle aged refugee women, simple Asian-style jackets, pants, ankle socks, and flip flops or bare feet*) _____

Chinese megaphone voice-over: _____

Marketplace of Korean refugees, merchants, and wounded soldiers _____
_____

SCENE 1: *THE NEWS*

Stage is set like a large backyard with a doorway and picnic table stage left and trees off to the side. Scene takes place on an afternoon in late August, 1950. The light on the back wall of the stage is warm and glowing.

Tony runs out to centre stage with a baseball mitt. He stands poised waiting for the ball to sail out, and it does! Once he catches it he has a few moments to talk to the audience before the rest of the players follow him.

Tony: When I caught that fly ball I knew the future – like Canada's – was mine. Our longest serving Prime Minister, William Lyon McKenzie King, had just died. Houses and factories were being built. Jobs and money were plentiful. Canada was finally getting back on its feet after the second world war. And most of all, that fly ball I caught had won the reunion game for Central High's graduating class of 1950!

"Reunion" – That's a laugh! We'd graduated only two months before and yet we'd seen each other just about every day all summer long. Looking back, I guess it did end up being our last reunion…with all of us, together, alive that is.

Mathieu had a scholarship for university – an Ivy Leaguer – which he deserved. Charlie and Brian were going to work in their grandfather's hardware store. And Digger and Vern were set on seeing the world. As for me, Tony, I was happy to get a job to help out my mom and sister.

Yup – the future was ours – problem was, it wasn't the future we expected.

A crowd of young men and women surge onto the performance space with coolers or picnic baskets. Half of the group clap Tony on the back and cheer his efforts and the other half good-naturedly tease him. Little sister Katie runs out and positions herself so that she catches the ball when Tony throws it to her. Mother enters through doorway and young women start setting the table. Young men carry out folding chairs or milk crates and sit on them. Groups of young people freeze in engaged positions of play and discussion.

Vern: Are you packed yet Mathieu?

Mathieu: Yeah, yeah. I've got the suitcase packed half full already. But would you look at this crummy sweater. And I still gotta get myself some socks! These ones got holes in them.

Digger: You better make sure they're nice and bright, eh! I heard they won't let you on campus if ya ain't got the right threads.

Mathieu: (*ruefully*) My scholarship is great and everything but it doesn't cover clothes, and boy do I need some new clothes! So what are you guys going to do anyway? Are you still planning on heading out of town in that souped up convertible?

Susan: (*shouting from the table where she is setting it*) Cruisin' for a bruisin' is more like it! (*everyone laughs and agrees*)

Vern: It's the wide world I'm itchin' to see. My oldest brother went on a tour of Europe right out of high school. Yeah, I know he was in the war and everything, but, (*shrugs*) the way he tells it, it was worth it. I can't wait to get out of this (*emphasis*) Nowheresville and hit the road.

Everyone shushes him and look in Tony's direction.

Tony: (*Acting cool-Tough, pleadingly*) Come on! I don't really mind. I gotta stay in town because I have to do the right thing. Unlike you carefree jokers I gotta be a real man. My dad was killed in the Second World War and we have his medals and everything, but… it's been hard on my mom …you know, having to work and raise Katie and me. Now we need money to fix the roof and get some things done before the house falls in. So, I guess it's my time to look after my family, just like my dad would have wanted. Problem is, I've got to find a good job real soon.

Irene has been listening. Comes over and gives his arm a little squeeze, and a smile. Then goes back into the house.

Charlie: Hey, I don't want to hear anybody knocking this town! Brian and I are staying and we're happy about it.

Brian: (*quickly cuts in*) Although I wouldn't mind seein' a few sights somewhere else. You know... I heard *Somewheresville's* supposed to be nice!

Other boys guffaw at his bad joke.

Charlie: We're going to be working in Grandad's hardware store and, who knows, maybe it'll be ours one day. But believe me, Tony, if we need to hire someone, you're it.

Digger: Yeah, but I know that Tony has the travelling' spirit too. And if it weren't for having to look after his mom and sis, I know he'd be coming with us. And get this. You know what Vern and I have been thinking of doing? (*Digger and Vern nod in agreement.*) Heading down to the States to join the American infantry fighting in Korea.

Brian: Korea, where's Korea?

Digger: Hey, don't you know nothing? It's a tropical country in Asia. (*pauses*) Yeah, it's got lot's of hot sun, beaches, palm trees….

Mathieu: Uhhh, I wouldn't exactly call it tropical Digger.

Charlie: Digger don't know much about Korea.

Tony: (*teasing him*) Yeah, but Digger knows a lot about babes.

Digger: You bet I do! Knowing about "Babes" is the most important thing a guy could ever do. And all the babes I know happen to like a man in a uniform. Especially a man who'll send them gifts from Korea.

Tony: I heard the war in Korea isn't going to last too long. Didn't it start because the North Koreans wanted to join with their countrymen from South Korea and unify it?

Digger: A little togetherness ain't a bad idea, is it? You know, getting cozy and all...

Tony: I wouldn't call it cozy Digger. The Americans are on one side of the divide, and the Russians and the Chinese are on the other. They set it up that way after they kicked-out the Japanese in 1945 at the end of the war.

Mathieu: The North Koreans want to unify the country. Problem is, they're doing it with Russian supplied weapons and communist ideas. The United States doesn't like that and neither does the United Nations.

Vern: The United Nations is trying to get us Canadians to join the fight. They're saying that if we don't stop the Communists, who will?

Brian: That's Vern all over, always the schoolyard policeman!

Irene: (*rushes out of the house*) Big news! Big news! They're even interrupting the top 10! (*fiddles with the radio as it makes static, then the station is found*)

Voice over of Announcer: We interrupt this broadcast to bring you an important announcement from Prime Minister St. Laurent. He is in our CBC studio in Ottawa. Go ahead, Prime Minister.

Prime Minister: Fellow Canadians. Today, on August 7, 1950, the government has authorized the recruitment of an additional army brigade which is beginning on Wednesday. (*gasps and surprise*) This brigade will be known as the Canadian Army Special Force. This brigade will be available for service in Korea as part of the United Nations forces. The United Nations action in Korea is not war. It is a police action intended to prevent war by discouraging aggression. (*nod heads*)

The brigade will be known as the Canadian Army Special Force. The infantry units will be organized as second battalions of the Royal Canadian Regiment, the Princess Patricia's, and the Royal 22nd Regiment.

The army wants young men, physically fit, mentally alert, single or married, and particularly just as many veterans of the Second World War as possible.

Scene 1: The gang listens to the CBC announcement.

All are frozen. Mother comes out in apron and wipes her hands on her apron, listening intently. She is shocked as she realizes what is in store. She runs to the radio and angrily turns it off.

Mom: Those leaders ought to be ashamed of themselves. Using young men – kids really – to fight their wars. Boys… you pay that radio no mind! (*Stomps back into the house.*)

Vern: You heard the Prime Minister, Mrs. Flahive. This ain't no war, it's a police action to prevent war. Looks to me like it's a great chance to see the world and get paid for it.

Mathieu: And a chance to keep the world safe from Communism!

Brian and Charlie: (*giving each other a high five and speaking in tandem*) Yah! A quick trip to *Somewheresville* and then home again! Woo Hoo!

Digger: And by getting myself a uniform and heading over to Korea, I am going to be the King of Babe Magnets. Just watch me!

Tony: And with a good paying job too!

Mother: What you young fools mean is that families across Canada are going to have to watch their boys go off and be killed again. And for what? (*scolding*) Let's not hear another word about it. Now, let's join hands for grace.

The group gathers round the table. Those in the centre circle hold hands. The others stand with hands clasped. All bow their heads.

Mother: Thank you for your gifts of shelter and food, of love and life, and friendship. May we use them to make the world a better place.

Katie: And Dear Lord, please keep Tony and his friends…safe from harm. (*Runs over to him and gives him a big hug. All are silent.*)

Curtains down.

Percussion Group: *military drum beat*

SCENE 2: *RECRUITMENT CENTRE*

(Table to stage right. Bookshelf. Office look.)

Officer 1: (*rubbing hands enthusiastically*) At last our government has given us the go ahead to go to Korea and help out with what has to be done.

Col. Jim Stone: The politicians are bowing to public and international pressure to become involved again on the world stage, but what the public doesn't realize, is how old our equipment is, and how few soldiers we actually have in our professional army.

Officer 1: Jim, you're just a pessimist.

Col. Stone: A pessimist, eh? Well maybe you can tell me how we're supposed to fight in the Korean terrain with the equipment we have and so few trained soldiers?

Officer 1: What's the problem? We'll climb a few mountains, scale a few ridges – just like Italy back in the '40's.

Col. Stone: More like Hong Kong in '41 you mean. They brought us in to shore up some British regiments, and then hung us out to dry. We were slaughtered by the Japanese. I know too many soldiers who still haven't recovered from those prisoner of war camps to think we mightn't be making a big mistake in Korea.

Officer 1: Jim…

Col. Stone: I know we're not allowed to second guess our commanders, but what I want to know is this: Is this supposed to be a United Nations initiative sponsored by the U.S. or a U.S. initiative sponsored by the United Nations? You tell me.

Officer 1: Look, I don't know about all that Jim. The government has spoken and we have to do our duty. The way I look at it is this: "in for a penny, in for a pound." We'll just see whether the public agrees.

Col. Stone: No matter what happens, my men are not going to be used as sacrificial pawns in some foreign war. If we go as soldiers, we'll go as soldiers who get the training and support we need. There will be no young men led to slaughter if I have anything to do with it. (phone rings)

Col. Stone: Yes, Officer Jim Stone here. What's that? The drill yard is crowded with men waiting to enlist? Yes, alright, send them in. *(Two officers gaze at each other in amazement. Crowd starts to advance on the office out of backstage left, moving purposefully but not rushed and reach the table just as the curtain closes.)*

CHOIR: "*Goodnight Irene*" by Huddie Lead Belly Ledbetter

SCENE 3: *JIVE GOODBYE*

Community centre party. Long tables with table cloths, chip bowls, and drinks flank the stage. DJ stage left. A banner "OUR BOYS ARE OFF TO PROTECT OUR FREEDOM" is hung overhead. 1950's big band music is playing. The main six boys are in soldier uniforms.

Tony strolls in with Irene. Katie, dressed up with ribboned pigtails, ankle socks, and dress enters opposite side. She yanks on her dress and appears uncomfortable.

Irene: Tony, do you know how upset your mom is about you going off to Korea? Given the chance I'm sure she'd have pulled you out of line at the recruiting station. Too bad for her you just turned 18.

Tony: Yeah, I know Irene. She feels our family has already done enough for democracy, what with my dad dying in Holland at the end of World War Two. But this is different. *(confused)* No, maybe it's the same. I don't know. All I know is that the United Nations is calling for Canada's help and lots of guys are joining up. I know how mom feels, and I don't mean to upset her, but I gotta do what I think is right. Right now, what really matters to me is how you feel about it.

Irene: Tony, I….*(They are just leaning into each other when Katie comes up and stands close to them, not noticing they are sharing a private moment.)* Katie, don't you look lovely!

Katie: Can you believe it! Momma made me wear this stupid dress. I'd rather be climbing trees.

Tony: But sis you look so cute. *(She grimaces.)* And hey, that skirt is loose enough to give you some room to move. Come on let's dance!

Katie: No!

Tony: *(pleadingly)* Come on Katie! It's my last night before we ship out for training in Seattle, down in the U.S. And after that it's Korea. I'm here, and I wanna dance. How about it Sis? It could be your last chance for a while you know.

Katie relents and they head to the dance floor. Irene talks to friends.

Susan: It's going to be dullsville with the boys gone.

Lisa: You don't mean boys – you mean Digger.

Susan: Well . . . he is so cute in his uniform.

Lisa: Yeah, tell me about it.

Sheila: I think what they're doing is so fine. Fighting to keep the world safe when they could be safe at home, building the lives they always dreamed of.

Heather: Ain't it funny though? First our grandfathers, then our fathers, and now our boyfriends. Why can't we ever get a break from war?

Lisa: Here they are, going off to Korea when people are getting good jobs and making good money again. My dad says things have never been better. And the music these day is just swinging. They'll be giving all this up.

Susan: Well at least they're not giving up their "girls". Or this girl anyway. 'C'mon, lets make sure they don't forget us!

D.J.: Ladies and Gentlemen! Boys and Girls! It's time to get this party started!, Tonight we have some special guests in uniform, some of the coolest cats this town has ever seen. Let's show' em we know how to get things cookin'!

DANCE: JIVE DANCE to "*Swing the Mood"* by Glen Miller

Crowd stands around clapping and grooving. At the end of the dance, the D.J. herds everyone together to take a photo. The soldiers are all crowded in together at the front. A big flash goes off: Everyone freezes and the curtains close.

SCENE 4: *KOREA*

Part 1: Arrival

CHOIR: *"If I'd Known You Were Coming I'd Have Baked A Cake"* by Eileen Barton

Soldiers enter with large kit bags and guns slung over their shoulders. Following them is Bill Boss. Soldiers are disoriented and dazed by the sights around them. Soundtrack of crowded street scene, people, horns honking, animals. Part of the choral group could also be in the corner singing, "If I'd known you were coming I'd have baked a cake", as was indeed the case!

Digger: I appreciate the nice welcome and everything, but …. where the heck are we? I don't see any palm trees. And it's f-f-f-freezing.

Charlie: Are those mountains? Nobody said anything about mountains. Somebody tell me this is a joke.

Mathieu: They don't expect us to climb mountains with all this gear do they?

Brian: My Bren gun weighs 90 pounds. Am I supposed to carry my gear, my gun, and myself up those hills? And what's with this cold? I should have paid more attention in Geography class. *"Nowheresville"* sure looks good to me now.

Tony: (*in awe*) Yeah, this is Korea alright. One mountain after another. And they say the Chinese have an endless supply of soldiers up there – just waiting for us.

Vern: Wow, this town is packed. And look at all these refugees! My brother told me about the millions of refugees in Europe after the Second World War. He said they had a really hard time. Now I think I know what he meant.

Col. Jim Stone: (*Moves briskly past the soldiers and barks orders.*) Let's go men. The Chinese have entered the war on the North Korean side and we've got our work cut out for us.

(*Men noticeably straighten up and move off smartly.*)

Bill Boss: (*enters with his bag over his shoulder and a wooden crate under his arm*) Bill Boss here… I'm a war correspondent, a reporter if you like. It's my job to give you folks back in Canada the real story about what's going on here. (*opens crate to inspect goods*) Thank goodness my stash of scotch and rye arrived intact. It's not for me, unfortunately. I'll trade these babies for a jeep, a trailer, a tent or a generator – what ever it takes to get me to the front. And that's where I'm headed – to the front, with our soldiers. I'll move when they move and I'll eat what they eat. It's the only way to cover a war. And so help me that's exactly what I'm going to do – cover this war.

Part 2: BATTLE DANCE: A modern dance to discordant music to depict battle, which in this war, includes guerilla warfare.

Part 3: Kap'yong

Soldiers are on patrol entering the performance area from different directions through the gym/auditorium. They gather centre stage in a semi-circle facing the audience and mime the appropriate response to match the narrative being relayed. Panels reminiscent of conical hills covered in rice paddies and close up brush and fir trees might be part of the setting. Bill is placed stage right at a makeshift table typing on a machine while Katie and Irene are stage left reading the newspaper together as they respond emotionally to the text.

Bill Boss: Headline: Canuck Heroism. Date: April, 1951. Canadian forces had their first major engagement in the hills around Kap'yong. Just before midnight on Sunday, April 21, 1951, Chinese and North Koreans forces began a massive offensive to re-take Seoul.

Col. Stone: The Chinese fought extremely well in the dark,

Bill Boss: reported Colonel Stone,

Col Stone: They live in the dark. We live in the light. Enemy guns have light tracers that follow the paths of bullets. Ours don't. Suddenly, these grey shapes came out of the darkness. That's when the machine guns opened up.

Bill Boss: After units from the South Korean, Australian, and American forces withdrew from their positions, the Canadians were cut off and surrounded.

Vern: But Colonel Stone told us,

Col. Stone: Be steady. Fight on. Don't give way.

Vern: And that's exactly what we did. We held on. We fought on. There were 7,000 Korean and Chinese troops attacking us. There were eight enemy soldiers for every one of us. It was hell, but we held on.

Bill Boss: Said Private Vern Mitchell. Private Tony Flahive also added,

Tony: We could see the enemy coming in waves up the hill. Before an attack they would shout and blow whistles. (*sound effects*). We called on the UN forces – the New Zealanders – for artillery support. Within minutes, a barrage of shells came down. (*Soldiers suddenly*

crouch low, ducking and covering heads) The hill we were on was a sea of fire and smoke. We sheltered as best we could. There were shells screaming all around us, landing just outside our positions. I thought we'd never get out alive. And then all of a sudden it was over. When it cleared and we looked out – the enemy was gone. It was unbelievable!

Bill Boss: Surrounded and isolated, Col. Stone called for his troops to be re-supplied. The only way to do this was by air-drop.

Digger: After the barrage there was barely enough ammunition to go around. And we were really low on water and food too. Next thing I know, the sky was filled with huge parachutes loaded with pallets of supplies. We looked up and boy did we do a dance. Only thing was, they dropped those pallets so close I thought we'd get flattened like pancakes.

Bill Boss: Said Private Digger O'Donahue. What was truly amazing was that of the almost 100 air-drops made that day, only four fell outside the Canadian position.

Irene: On the afternoon of Wednesday April 25, 1951 the Chinese Communist forces that had attacked the Canadians at Hill 677 withdrew north. By all accounts this battle was crucial in stopping communist forces from taking the Korean capital of Seoul. To their credit, Canadian forces suffered only 10 killed and 23 wounded.

Brian: (*Increasingly panicky*) Charlie? Charlie? Has any one seen Charlie? Charlie! (*Breaks down and someone puts his arm around him.*)

Bill Boss: The 2nd Battalion of the Princess Patricia's Canadian Light Infantry was awarded the United States Presidential Distinguished Unit Citation. The only Canadian unit ever to have received this award. (*Soldiers slowly pull themselves to attention and stand tall. Lights blare on them and then dim.*)

MUSICAL INTERLUDE: *Traditional Korean Music*

Scene 4: The Battle of Kap'yong

SCENE 5: *SEOUL*

Curtain opens up on a group of wounded soldiers who are being tended to by a Red Cross nurse. Vern and Brian walk on carrying a stretcher, while Mathieu wheels a wounded soldier in. Outside of this group a small distance away are marketplace merchants and refugees, perhaps around a cooking pot. A ways off is Bill Boss, writing on a pad of paper while sitting on a crate. Pierre Berton is interviewing the Red Cross woman with a microphone and a tape recorder.

Pierre Berton: I can see Miss White that your work is invaluable. Can you tell me where you're from, and what you're up to?

Muriel White: My name is Muriel White. I grew up on a farm just up from Lake Ontario, near Elizabethville. Population: thirty-two. You know what they say: If you blink, you miss it. (*chuckles*) A cousin of my father suggested I might work for the Red Cross. And that's what I did. After a year or so I was transferred to a veteran's hospital in Toronto, where I was in arts and crafts. One day a supervisor asked me if might be interested in working in another part of the world, and since I've got a sense of adventure, I agreed. Next thing I know, here I am in an over-crowded hospital in the middle of Seoul, Korea. Talk about an adventure. (*She is summoned.*)

Pierre Berton: I wonder if you could tell me about what it's like ...

Muriel White: (*interrupting him as she rises*) Excuse me, Mr. Berton, I'm very sorry but I'm being called. I very much appreciate your interest in me and the work we do, but I am needed at the moment. (*turns to leave*) Yes, that's it..tell about the desperate needs here.

He nods his head and moves away and watches as she checks the body on the stretcher. She shakes her head, and the two boys carry the body off. He turns around and catches the view of Bill Boss. He is startled to see Bill, then walks over to him.

Bill crosses the stage looking at some papers.

Pierre Berton: Bill? Bill Boss! (*Bill looks up and they greet each other with great gusto.*) You old dog! You here too? The last time I saw you was at the Press Club supper back in Ottawa, wasn't it?

Bill Boss: Ha! Ha! Ha! And look at us now Pierre, in the middle of a war in Korea. Sure is a long way from Sparks Street isn't it? (*pauses and gets serious*) To tell you the truth, Pierre, I just got back from the front, and let me tell you, it's been tough . . . (*shakes head, cannot speak, and then bucks up*) Well, I'm sure looking forward to a bit of a clean-up. Going to get myself a shower as hot as I can stand it. What about you? What are you up to?

Pierre Berton: I just got in Bill. I'm on assignment with Maclean's Magazine. I suppose we're here for pretty much the same thing – to get a good story and send it home so that the armchair-sitters in Canada get some idea of what's really going on here.

Bill Boss: An armchair ... I've been here so long I almost forget what it's like to sit in an armchair. And let me tell you Pierre, this city is so wrecked I doubt you'd find a chair of any kind to sit on. Hey Tony! ...(*signals to his driver who is standing off to the side to join them*) Pierre, if any man in Korea deserves to sit himself down in an armchair this is him. This is my driver, Private Tony Flahive. And this is our translator – a chap we call "Dickie" – he's attached to the South Korean Army.

Pierre Berton: I'm pleased to meet you. Tell me Tony, have you seen much action?

Tony: I was with the Princess Pats up in Kapy'ong and all that, but they've decided to give us a break – so my buddies and I have been temporarily transferred to work behind the lines.

Pierre Berton: Maybe I could pick your brain sometime. You could help me get my feet wet – give me an idea of what's really going on here.

Tony: I'd be pleased to Sir, but we're assigned to accompany Mr. Boss, and so long as he doesn't object….

Bill Boss: No, no . . . That's fine Tony. Besides now's a good time for me to file my latest dispatch with the Canadian Press.

They nod in agreement and Bill Boss departs.

Tony: So what do you think of Korea, Mr. Berton.

Pierre Berton: I just got off the plane to tell you the truth. But one thing I've learned already is that if Korea was once known as "Land of the Morning Calm" it certainly isn't any more. You see, son, my job is to tell the truth. And what I'm planning is to file a series of stories that will make this war real for all the Canadians back home. Let's start with the Korean people... (*turns to the refugee group*)

Mrs. Tak: Sir, you please buy something. Beautiful bracelet from my grandmothers great grandmother. Last thing left to trade for rice.

Dickie: This place now look only like broken wood and brick. But it is our city. This is the home-place for my country. We have been attacked four times since the last nine months.

Mrs. Tak: Two times the North Korean and Chinese forces come, and two times the United Nations forces push them back. Enemy takes everything sir, every piece of china, furniture, cloth, and all food.

Dickie: Only thing they leave in my house is book. I think enemy is ignorance, and cannot read. This is ancient city, and we have seen many troubles, but this city, my home, will survive.

Pierre Berton: What of this woman's family?

Dickie: I know her. Speak to her many times while passing to army compound. Watched children die. Her family lived in north but had to walk over mountains in winter snow to come here for safety.

Mrs. Tak: My husband taken by Communist to march North and work in field while soldiers fighting. My many children died. Only baby, my mother and sister now.

Sister: There is much sickness and hunger here, but we people come to this home-place because our villages burned and our rice crops gone and the war is killing us. Too many, too many bombs...

Dickie: There are many such stories. Too many such stories. Thank you to Canadians and United Nations forces for coming to help us.

Dickie and Tony clasp hands. Curtains close. Katie steps in front of the curtains at centre stage.

Scene 5: Seoul. Pierre Berton interviews Mrs. Tak and family

Katie: (*in dress*) Dear Tony: Its Sunday December 8, 1951. I hate Sundays. Momma won't let me go running or climb trees on Sundays. We went to church this morning, and then there was nothing else to do all day. So guess what? I decided to start a scrapbook with each weeks' news about the war until you come home. I started with Friday's newspaper because it had the headline, "Price Legislation Leading to Christmas Sales War." I cut it out, but Mama said it had nothing to do with the war in Korea. The only other thing I could find was on page 5. It said, (*opens scrapbook*), "Canadian's Chinese Saves The Day." It said that Jacques Morin, from the Van Doos Regiment, learned to speak some Chinese from his neighbours in Toronto when he was a boy. Anyway, he was up on Hill 355, and he was listening to the enemy's radio transmissions and he could understand what they were saying. By golly, he kept tricking them and bringing up soldiers where the Chinese least expected them! Tony, I know there are Korean soldiers fighting alongside you. Are you learning Korean? I hope the Koreans appreciate you. Then it will make missing you not so bad.

SCENE 6: *NIGHT PATROL*

Scene starts out dimly lit. Vern, Brian, Mathieu, Digger, and Tony are taking a break from night patrol stage left, when mega-phone voice-over is heard.

Chinese megaphone voice: (*expressively, persuasively*) Canadian soldier. This not your land. This is not your people. Why you fight this war? Family is waiting for you at home. Childrens is missing you. Maybe girlfriend or wife has new boyfriend. Do not stay here and fight Canadian soldier. Put gun down and go home. It not your problem.

Digger: (*getting worked up, starts to whisper out loud*) Hey, maybe your girl's got herself a new boyfriend, but my Susan never would!

Vern: Digger, don't shout for Pete's sakes! You'll give away our position.

Mathieu: That's just the Chinese propaganda machine wasting their time. They're trying to get you all worked up. So don't let' em.

Tony: Yeah, we'll be working alright. Working up and working down that there hill. Like my friend David Cathcart used to say: life at the front is 90% boredom and 10% pure terror. Let's just hope tonight it's 90% boredom.

Brian: What hill are we patrolling tonight?

Tony: Orders are Hill 162.

Brian: That's a relief. It's only 162 feet high. Remember Hill 667? That one just about killed me. This war is all about patrolling, and not much else. It's static. It's like we're stuck in the same routine: up the hill on one side, and down the hill on the other. I feel like Jack and Jill.

Digger: C'mon guys. Each night brings us a little closer to home.

Vern: Digger, it's not like you to be so thoughtful.

Digger: I've been listening to Tony talk about Irene…and I've been re-reading Susan's letters. I'm thinking of putting away my little black address book and asking Susan to be my only girl. (*All the boys tease him a bit.*)

Mathieu: Wow! If Digger can settle down with only one girl, then miracles do happen. And who knows, maybe those peace talks might end up in a ceasefire after all!

MUSICAL INTERLUDE: *Percussion group performance emphasizing a variety of wind and rain sounds. Near the end there is a sniper gunshot and Digger falls. As curtains are closing, Katie steps out holding her scrapbook – more grown up but maintaining her tomboy spirit.*

Katie: January 10, 1953. Dear Tony, There was very little about Korea in the paper today. I hate to say it, but there appears to be less and less. It seems the only people interested in the war nowadays are those of us waiting for you boys to come home. I know there's some peace talks going on, but the end doesn't seem in sight. Anyway, I cut out the photo of Able Seaman Mark Draibye of Montreal "greeting" Shirley Dowling of Halifax just after his ship the HMCS Iroquois arrived home from Korean waters. (*scandalized*) You know what? He had his lips pressed right on hers! I heard Irene and Digger's girlfriend saying that's just how they plan to greet you and Digger when you get home. Mom got a hold of the picture and took it away from me though. Oh, and by the way, there was this article in the paper about the movie star Humphrey Bogart getting into trouble with his neighbours because his dog was barking too much. He said, "I will defend to the death the right of any dog to bark. Freedom of speech should extend not merely to humans." That got me thinking, Tony. It seems silly to me they should be writing in the paper about Humphrey Bogart's freedom fight, and not yours.

SCENE 7: *HOMECOMING*

Curtains open partially to reveal a disheveled Bill Boss sitting at his typewriter.

Bill Boss: (*triumphant*) Date: July 27, 1953. Headline: Korean Armistice Declared. Location: Panmunjom, Korea. After two years, two weeks and three days of negotiations the UN and the Communist delegations signed their names to an armistice agreement. Even so, the combatants continued shooting at each other until ten o'clock last night. (*shakes head*). After that, both sides fired off what remained of their ammunition in a random fashion. A human sea of Chinese soldiers stood across the valley, waving flags and shouting. (*wonderment*) I guess they are just as glad to go home as we are. (*Tearfully puts head in hands as if to cry. Curtains close*)

The sound of a train whistle as the four boys enter from stage right: Charlie and Digger are of course missing. Waiting to greet them are Mother, Irene, Katie and Susan. Katie and Irene break into a run and hug Tony. Then the other guys shake Irene's hand or make an affectionate gesture (tousling hair, patting back) to the grown up Katie.

Tony's mother hangs back with Susan. Then he breaks free of the crowd and goes towards her. They stand looking at each other and then she embraces him.

Mom: (*happily*) You're home. Home at last! Thank God you're safe!

All the boys: Home. Yeah, we're home. Safe.

Susan who has been standing back, steps forward.

Susan: (*hopefully*) Digger? Where's Digger?

Mathieu: I'm sorry Susan, it happened just before the Armistice was signed. We thought it best if we told you ourselves. . .

She drops her head and collapses emotionally. All support her as they move offstage.

Left on-stage are: Tony, Vern, Katie, and Irene.

Tony: I can't believe we're finally home, about to pick up the future where we left off.

Vern: (*looking around*) Is this a joke? Are you the only folks who've come out to meet us? When my brother came back from the Second World War the station was crowded with people. There were brass bands, flags, speeches – everything. Where is everybody?

Tony: (*bewildered*) It's like they said. Nobody noticed. Nobody cared.

Irene: Tony, that's not true. There may not be a lot of people here tonight, and maybe a lot of people were too busy to really know what went on over in Korea, but you must believe that we were with you every step of the way – in our hearts and in our minds. And we thank God you're home safe.

Katie: So what was it all about really? How will it make the world a better place? How is it supposed to give us a more secure future?

Vern: When it started, the politicians told us it was about keeping the world free from communism and dictatorships.

Tony: All I know is, I went to war because my country called me, the same way my dad answered the call against the Nazi's in Europe, or the millions of others around the world who joined up against the Fascists in Asia and Africa. This time it was Korea. Next time, who knows?

Katie: Well let's hope there is no next time. Our leaders asked you to go and you went. Good for you and good for Canada. But it makes me realize how important it is that we choose our leaders carefully. Anyone who thinks we can make the world a better place by having more and more wars is not the kind of leader I want. Maybe the time has come for people like us to become the leaders.

Tony: For three years 27,000 Canadians were deadlocked in Korea. Twenty-seven thousand is a lot of people who joined up from a lot of little *Nowheresvilles* like ours. I only hope this country doesn't forget who we were and what we did.

Irene: I know the South Koreans certainly will remember.

Vern: Yeah, you're right. And while we won't forget, at last it's time to remember how to live in peace.

Curtains close.

CHOIR: *"Let There Be Peace on Earth"* by Jill Jackson and Sy Miller, circa 1955

SCENE 8: *CEREMONY OF REMEMBRANCE*

*Curtains open onto the stage set with a Commonwealth War Graves Commission style headstone. The actors stand evenly spaced, two on one side and two on the other across the front of the stage. See **Teacher's Guide: Ceremony of Remembrance** for additional details and procedures.*

Vern: The story we lived today tells the tale of the approximately 27,000 Canadians who served in the Korean conflict. Of this number, 516 gave their lives and 1,042 were injured. While the numbers of dead and casualties do not compare with the thousands upon thousands of Canadians who were killed or injured in the First and Second World Wars, these men and women – like the millions who went before them – joined up prepared to make the ultimate sacrifice. Their bravery and willingness to sacrifice should never be forgotten.

Irene: Overall, this war initiated a number of tragic firsts for the world. The first time the chemical napalm was used. The first time jet aircraft played a major part in a war. The first shots fired in what became the Cold war between the Democratic West and the Communistic East – a costly and dangerous stalemate that divided the world and lasted for almost half a century.

Tony: It also constituted a positive first for Canada. This was the first time military action was taken under the umbrella of the United Nations. This planted the seed for the idea that Mike Pearson, Canada's 14th Prime Minister and winner of a Nobel Peace Prize, later developed: that of a United Nations Peacekeeping force to resist aggression. In many ways, the soldiers of the Korean War were the first in a long line of Canadian peacemaking or peacekeeping missions.

Katie: And so, today, on November 11th, we remember the brave men and women who helped make us who we are by their participation in war and peacekeeping.

Vern: We remember with pride those who fought bravely and selflessly.

Katie: We remember with affection and sadness those cut down in the promise of their youth or the richness of their middle life.

Vern: We remember with gratitude all of those Canadians who went before,

Tony: Whose contribution to the cause of freedom in Two World Wars, the Korean War, and several United Nations Peacekeeping and UN sanctioned NATO Peacemaking missions, shaped our country and the world today.

Irene and Katie: We remember the terrible cost of war. Let us use that knowledge to guide us towards peace.

Together: Together we remember. And we thank you.

The Honour March takes place to music which is solemn but moving, like "Hymn to the Fallen" from the movie "Saving Private Ryan."

Once the wreathe is laid that same person asks the audience to:

"PLEASE STAND"

- **BUGLE CALL: The Last Post**

- **MOMENT OF SILENCE**

- **The moment of Silence is ended when the wreathe-layer says, "Please join us in the singing of 'O Canada'."**

- **All sing "O Canada."**

Curtains close. The performance and Ceremony of Remembrance is ended.

Scene 7: Homecoming

A TRIO OF WARS: A GIFT OF PEACE

A Play and A Ceremony

Suitable for Performance by: Grades 4 to 8

Plot Summary:

Three Storytellers, who are suggestive of angels or a modern version of "Father Time" follow three families through the First, Second, and Korean Wars, highlighting the similarities and differences between the experiences. The play is visually organized along a timeline with the action for each era and family occurring at the same spot on the stage. The conversation between the storytellers is interspersed to clarify historical details as well as articulate general ideas about war and peace at a level appropriate for children.

The three family groupings introduced in **_Scene 1: The Call to Enlist_** include a WWI family whose university-bound son willingly goes off to what is expected to be a short and adventurous war; a WWII working class family whose carpenter father joins the army due to a growing worry that Hitler and Hirohito will overcome us all; and a 1950's picnicking family whose son joins up for Korea in memory of his father who died in WWII. The choir sings *"It's a Long Way to Tipperary."*

Scene 2: The Reasons Why has the three storytellers comparing the world to a playground and the differing contexts of the wars to age-appropriate playground examples. This scene ends in a stomp-inspired "Bully Dance" symbolizing the fascist bullies of WWII.

The men who signed up in Scene 1 re-appear in **_Scene 3: The War Front_** where each group emphasizes what the war is like for them, mentioning details of particular battles or aspects of the battlefields specific to that war.

Scene 4: The Home Front explores the deprivations, efforts and worries of those assisting the war effort from afar. The choir opens the scene with *"Keep the Home Fires Burning."* The scene ends with the cessation of hostilities and the gift of peace. Of the three men, the Korean soldier safely returns home, the WWII father is seriously wounded and the WWI son's death is symbolized by the delivery of the telegram and broken watch delivered to his mother.

The Storytellers briefly discuss the active meaning of "peace" from a child's perspective and lead the **_Scene 5: Ceremony of Remembrance_**. All the Cast and Crew enter the stage during the Honour March to solemn but moving music. The laying of the wreathe is followed by the Last Post and the Moment of Silence, which ends with the singing of "O Canada."

Acting Roles:

Speaking Roles: 28 individual roles

Group scenes for additional non-speaking roles:
- marketplace opening
- soldiers in the wars
- factory workers
- telegram delivery man

Music/Choral Options:

Choir: *"It's a Long Way to Tipperary"* by Jack Judge and Harry Williams

Choir: *"Till the Boys Come Home"* (*Keep the Home Fires Burning*) by Lena Guilbert Ford and Ivor Novello

Choir: *"Une Colombe"* by Celine Dion

Honour March: *"Hymn to the Fallen"* from the movie *"Saving Private Ryan"*

Dance Options:

"No Man's Land Waltz" : a modern dance to jolting instrumental music emphasizing the madness of trench warfare, and the tragedy of this war in particular.

[Previous performances: Rockcliffe Park P.S. Ottawa, Ontario. Directed by Barbara Brockmann (2005, 2008); WWI Scenes at the Sunset Ceremony, Vigil 1914-1918 Project, National War Memorial, November 10, 2008]

CHARACTERS AND COSTUMES

In order of appearance. Roles with full names are based on real people.
Use the character list below to record the names of your cast members!

Opening Market Scene, WWI: *Actors are dressed in WWI clothing styles. This is a flexible scene which can be packed with as many or few actors you have available.*

Newspaper Boy: _____

Enlistment Officers: _____

Market Sellers: _____

Singers: _____

Scenario Groups:

a) **"Look for the good" Group:** (*children playing with a ball*) _____
_____

b) **"Be welcoming" Group:** (*children with school books*) _____
_____

c) **"Accept responsibility" Group:** (*adults passing in the marketplace*) _____
_____

d) **"Be generous" Group:** (*apple vendor and two to three shabbily dressed children*) _____
_____

e) **"Think for yourself" Group:** (*3 workers carrying lumber or briefcases, and a few officers at an enlistment table*) _____
_____

f) **"Solve problems with words" Group:** _____
_____

Storytellers:

Storyteller 1: _____
Storyteller 2: _____
Storyteller 3: _____

The storytellers are dressed in shades of white and beige. They can be male or female, and their clothes might be layered robes or modern yet simple styles. They should be vaguely reminiscent of modern angels or "Father Time."

WWI Scenes:

This is a prosperous upper middle class bilingual family whose son is going off to university. In the <u>Scene 1</u> *they are dressed in stylish clothes of 1914: in* <u>Scene 4</u> *Maman has a shawl, Bettina is in a well-worn (dirtied, and possibly bloodied) nurse's "bluebird" uniform, and Mathilde is wearing overalls and carrying a rake.*

Maman: (*motherly*) _____
Bettina: (*earnest*) _____
Mathilde: (*energetic*) _____
Papa: (*supportive*) _____
George: (*enthusiastic*) _____
Soldier 1: (*tired*) _____
Soldier 2: (*angry*) _____
Soldier 3: (*intelligent*) _____

WWII Scenes:

This is a comfortable working class family who has just experienced financial success after the hard times of the Depression. Clothing styles are late 1930's.

Mother: (*anxious*) _____

Father: (*determined*) _____

Hannah: (*younger sister, teasing*) _____

Jack: (*brother, single minded*) _____

Soldier 4: _____

Soldier 5: _____

Soldier 6: _____

Factory girls wear baggy jeans or overalls underneath matching black aprons or simple grey cotton tunics. Hair is tied up under colourful bandana's like "Rosie the Riveter" style. They may mime or carry a variety of items like a straw broom, pail, hammer, screwdriver or large funnel.

Factory Girl 1: (*worried*) _____

Factory Girl 2: (*dreamy*) _____

Factory Girl 3: (*defiant*) _____

Factory Girl 4: (*worried*) _____

Factory Girl 5: (*enthusiastic*) _____

Korean War Scenes:

This is a comfortable middle class family. Clothing styles are 1950's summer.

Mom: (*determined*) _____

Tina: (*demonstrating a comfortable teasing relationship between siblings*) _____

Joe: (*young man, recent graduate*) _____

Murray: (*friend of Joe*) _____

Soldier 7: _____

Soldier 8: _____

Scene 1: The Call to Enlist

SCENE 1: *THE CALL TO ENLIST*

The play is staged in three distinct locations: stage right, centre, and stage left. In this way, the three wars of Canadian participation that we honour on Remembrance Day are viewed like a timeline continuum: WWI, WWII, and the Korean War. Unless otherwise indicated, the action of each particular war always takes place in the same area of the stage

Newspaper boy enters apron of stage (closed curtains) as George and Papa enter the other side.

Newspaper Boy: (*shouting*) Today's Ottawa Citizen* for Sale! Get your Ottawa Citizen! Headline: Would-Be Soldiers Line Up Around The Block on Elgin Street. First Canadian Battalion Rushes to Mother England's Side. (**Use name of your local prominent newspaper.*)

Papa: We'll take one!

They look at it, look at each other, and rush off.

The scene unfolds as a market place crowd pours into the front of the "performance space" from any available door. Adult roles, like enlistment officers, market sellers, and shoppers enter from side. Child roles come in singing in a kind of parade from the back through the audience. Once the "marketplace" or town square feeling is established, the tableau freezes for the duration of each performance. In between there is movement and noise. The timing between each group is both natural yet tightly timed.

Singers: (*same tune as French folk-song, "Napoléon avait cinq cents soldats"*)
Les Canadiens avaient cinq cents soldats,
Les Canadiens avaient cinq cents soldats,
Les Canadiens avaient cinq cents soldats,
Marchant d'un même pas !

Mama steps out from the curtains.

Maman: Mathilde! Bettina! Je vous cherche! Le temps est arrive!

Mathilde and Bettina: Bien sur Maman!

Singers: Aurevoir!

Singers join the choir. One of them who has been throwing a ball in the air "accidentally" puts it down in a central location to wave goodbye and forgets it. She joins another group while Mathilde and Bettina join their mother shopping for apples.

"Look for the good" Group:

A child finds the ball and starts bouncing it, humming "Les Canadiens." The ball owner sees this, runs over. The other group of children watch carefully.

Can I have my ball back?

> Uh, oh...it's yours? Sure! (*hands it over—child runs to protective coverage as other group moves menacingly close.*)

Hey, why did you steal my sister's ball?

> What are you talking about? (*confused*) I didn't steal it. I found it on the ground.

Sure, sure. You're such a liar.

> I'm not a liar.

I saw you take it. You were going to keep it. You'd better watch out.

> I didn't take it! I found it. Why do you guys always try to stir up trouble? You always look for the bad in people.

"Be welcoming" Group:

One child is standing alone while others are grouped together peering in her direction..

Look at her. She's that new girl in our class.

> She's a stranger. And she doesn't look like us.

What do you mean? I think she looks like us.

> No. Look, her hair is curly (*straight, long, short, whatever hair the actor has!*).

And besides, she doesn't sound like us.

> Ohhhhh, that's true.

Like I said, she's a stranger.

> Ahhhhh (*understanding the implication now*)

Child notices them staring at her. She walks shyly over, and speaks in the accent and grammar of an immigrant group in your community

Hello. I know your face. You live on my street don't you?

> Oh yes, that's right.

Can I play with you?

> No-o-o, I don't think so. We have better things to do. (*They arrogantly walk away.*)

"Accept responsibility" Group:

Two adults passing

Sir, when you drove your new fangled automobile down our street last week you frightened my horse. Would you please drive at a reduced speed?

> Well your horse will just have to get used to it. I can't be responsible for your horse's nerves. Or your nerves for that matter. Good day to your Sir.

"Be generous" Group:

Apple vendor is bothered by shabbily dressed children lingering close at hand.

> What is it child? You've been hanging around all day, bothering my customers.

We, we, ….

    Well, what is it. Speak up.

We're hungry. Could we have an apple?

    So that's what you're after is it? Free food! No! There are jobs to be had if you'd just apply yourself. The mill is looking for workers, and you could always shine shoes or sell newspapers. Earn your own keep…If you think I'm going to give you some of my hard earned money you're crazy? Now, SKEDDADLE!

"Think for yourself" Group:

Officers: Join up now! Help our Allies beat the enemy! Be a man and stand beside Mother England when she needs you! Your country needs you!

Worker 1: I'm thinking of enlisting

Worker 2: Whatever for?

Worker 1: I want some adventure in my life. I want an opportunity to travel, to see a bit of the world.

Worker 2: Believe me, you won't be doing much travelling far from a battlefield.

Worker 3: I'm going to protect England. She's like our mother country. And the fighting is happening in France. It's like he's our father. You wouldn't leave your parents defenseless, would you?

Worker 2: Well no-o-o-o, but what about the actual fighting? Why would you kill fellas you don't even know, for a squabble that doesn't even concern us! It makes no sense to me.

Worker 2: You know Frank, you can say what you like, but if you don't enlist, people will think you're a coward. Plain and simple.

Worker 3: That's right Frank, a coward.

Worker 1: So Frank, are you coming to enlist with us?

Worker 2: Well…(*thoughtfully*) I guess you're right about that. I suppose I don't have much of a choice do I? All right, let's go…. (*They head towards the line up.*)

"Solve problems with words" Group:

Children standing in a circle playing a handclapping game are accidentally interrupted by an exuberant pair chasing each other. As the groups collide, everyone collapses in a splendid heap.

Hey! What are you doing?

    Whaddya mean?

You hurt us.

    Huh, Huh (*confusion*)…You're wrong! It's the other way around! YOU hurt US! Well, we're not puttin' up with you fellas knockin' us over.

Both "sides": (*each word emphasized with pointed fingers*) THIS IS WAR!

(*At the exact moment their mutual glare is about to erupt in a fight, a parading choir marches through and the crowd disperses as the choir sings.*)

CHOIR: "*It's a Long Way to Tipperary*" by Jack Judge and Harry Williams

The three storytellers enter the performance space carrying a simple poster with the date and name of their war clearly printed on it. They attach it along the apron of the stage during the singing and wait until they are alone.

Storyteller 1: War. Yes, the root of war goes back to a time before even I can remember.

Storyteller 3: Sadly, the root of war starts growing whenever people think they are better than others.

Storyteller 2: It blooms whenever someone deliberately thinks the worst of others and stirs up trouble.

Storyteller 3: It happens when people cannot accept differences or be tolerant and welcoming.

Storyteller 1: Or can't solve problems with the appropriate words or say sorry.

Storyteller 3: Or do not accept responsibility for their actions.

Storyteller 2: This is the story of all wars in general, and three wars in particular. These are not the only wars Canadians have participated in, but they are the wars which have touched us most deeply in the last hundred years.

Storyteller 1: Canadians don't go to war easily. We are not greedy for other people's land or riches. Canadians believe that conflict can be solved by other means than war.

Storyteller 3: But if someone needs help, we'll consider it, and if it seems just, we'll pitch in and do our part.

Storyteller 1: Each of these wars took place at a different time. The Great War, as it was known at first, was fought from 1914 to 1918. It was also called, "The war to end all wars"….Honestly!...It was a World War and it was the biggest war that had ever been fought up to that point. It affected so many people in so many countries, and there was so much killing and terrible destruction, that everyone thought it was the war to end all wars, until…..

Storyteller 2: ...until the Second World War, that is! It was called World War Two, and it took place from 1939 to 1945.

Storyteller 1: When people realized that this was a second world war, and that it once again involved a huge number of people from all six continents, well that's when the name of the Great War was changed to the First World War...

Storyteller 3: ...and the third war in our trio of wars was not a world war, but still powerful for those who experienced it. It was the Korean War.

Storyteller 2: What were all those wars about? What is any argument in your family or with your friends about? A difference of opinion that grows bigger and bigger until it swallows everybody up with its own crazy reasons.

Storyteller 3: The story of war is the story of families: the families in your neighbourhood, the families on the "other side", and maybe, just maybe, your own family.

Curtains open to reveal three separate groups. WWI family is admiring a group of singers, WWII family is gathered around the kitchen table with children doing homework while Mother washes and shines a bowl of apples, and the Korean War group is listening to the radio in a picnic setting. Each group freezes in their tableau setting when not performing.

CHOIR grouping again: *"It's a Long Way to Tipperary" (Second verse)*

WWI Family:

Clapping as they turn away from the choir who then disperse offstage.

Maman: What a catchy tune! (*As she turns away, Mathilde tries to sneak an apple from behind her.*) Hey, (*teasingly*) you little monkey! Here (*throws her one*). Next time be sure to ask, ok?

Bettina: They've been singing that song all over England for some time. Now it's catching on in Canada as our boys head off to war.

Maman: I know war between England and Germany has been declared, but Canada has been a country of our own for almost 40 years now. We're not a colony of England anymore. So, pourquoi? Why should we get involved in a war that is over the seas and doesn't concern us?

Mathilde: Maman, you are the only person I know who thinks that way! We have to stand beside Mother England and France. These are our closest allies and Canada must lend a hand.

Maman: (*checking her timepiece*) Where is that father and brother of yours?

Papa: Here we are!

Maman: Your final farewell moments with us before you leave for university, and you arrive late as usual!

Mathilde: Get a move on George or you'll miss your train. I can't wait to see a steam train up close!

George: Sorry Maman, I…I won't need to go the train station today.

Maman: Why George? Did you manage to get yourself a ride in one of those new motor coaches instead?

George: No Maman. It's just that…well, I've signed up.

Bettina: Signed up? Signed up for what? A different university?

George: No, I've signed up, I've enlisted in the army. I'm going to fight overseas.

Maman: No! You're barely old enough George! Papa, you can't agree to this!

Papa: (*sympathetically*) I'm sorry Dear, but he is old enough. Actually, I went down with him to enlist myself, but they turned me down. Said I was too old to fight. So I volunteered to take a desk job so I could help out any way I can.

Mathilde: George, what luck! Promise me you'll write to us about every single adventure!

Papa: (*persuasively*) Now, now dear. I'm sure it will only be for a few months. Darling, consider it part of his education. Everyone says the war will be over by Christmas. He'll have an adventure and before we know it he'll be back to school in the spring!

Maman: (*sigh*) Alright then. George, I'll give you my timepiece. Whenever you look at it, you'll think of your dear Maman and know that we'll be together again before this watch stops ticking.

Freeze. **WWII Family Group** *is activated.*

Mother is standing at a centre table shining apples as she moves them from the basket to the bowl. The two children are doing homework.

Mother: You KNOW what 7 times 9 are. We went over this yesterday.

Jack: (*mutters*) 60,….no…..62…..no…63! 7 times 9 are sixty three!

Hannah: Let's see, Canada became the Dominion of Canada in…1867. If its 1939 now, we've been a country for how many years?

Jack: I can figure it out!

Hannah: Sure you can! Have a go at it mister math genius!

Mother: Children! That's enough! Father will be hungry and tired after a hard day's work and I don't want him to see you two arguing. (*door slams*)

Father: Hello all! (*hugs daughter who notices clean clothes*)

Hannah: Daddy, you're not dirty at all. Weren't you working today?

Father: I …I spent the day in the line-up.

Mother: (*panicking*) Line-up? What line-up? I thought there was plenty of work for you this year. Why were you in a line-up?

Father: Not the employment line up dear, the enlistment line up.

Jack: Dad! You're going to fight overseas!

Mother: No! What will we do without you?

Father: We all have to do our part. We have to. We can't let those devils Hirohito and Hitler take over the world. I know the war seems far away right now, but it won't be if we don't do something about it.

FREEZE…. **Korean War Family** is activated. Joe and Tina grab an apple and throw it to the other. They do this back and forth a few times, laughing and teasing each other.

Mom: Hey! Give me back that apple! There won't be enough apples for everyone if you use them like footballs!

Joe: Actually, we were thinking more like baseballs.

Mom: As long as you don't use them for hockey pucks!

Tina: Hey, now that's a great idea… She shoots, she scores! (*Takes a big bite!*)

Mom: Sports and more sports. It's a wonder you were able to graduate from high school with all the sports you do. But you did. (*Mom unpacks picnic lunch while the kids throw an apple back and forth for each phrase spoken.*)

Joe: And with honours I might add!

Tina: What a fluke. The secretary's pen slipped!

Joe: Let's hope the same dame is working when you graduate!

Tina: Just you wait, Joe! My goal is to beat you by winning every scholarship you ever applied for!

Mom: Enough now! If only you two would compete when it comes to getting your chores done on time!

Murray: (*rushes in with a transistor radio*) Hi Mrs. Howell! You won't believe the news.

Joe: You won't believe our news! Mom bought tickets for the family to go on a trip to Montreal before I leave for university.

Murray: Wow, that's great, but this news is even bigger. The Prime Minister is on the radio making an announcement.

Tina: Here, I'll turn it on!

Radio Announcer: We interrupt this broadcast to bring you an important public service announcement from Prime Minister St. Laurent. He is in our CBC studio in Ottawa. Go ahead, Prime Minister

Prime Minister Louis S. Laurent: Fellow Canadians. Today, on August 7, 1950, the government has authorized the recruitment of an additional army brigade which is beginning on Wednesday. This brigade will be known as the Canadian Army Special Force. This brigade will be available for service in Korea as part of the United Nations forces. The United Nations action in Korea is not war. It is police action intended to prevent war by discouraging aggression.

The brigade will be known as the Canadian Army Special Force and it will be specially trained and equipped to be available for use in carrying out Canada's obligations under the United Nations charter. The infantry units will be organized as second battalions of the Royal Canadian Regiment, the Princess Patricia's, and the Royal 22nd Regiment. The association of the new brigade with these historic regiments will have numerous advantages.

The army wants young men, physically fit, mentally alert, single or married, and particularly just as many veterans of the Second World War as possible.

Murray: My oldest brother fought in Europe during World War Two. He always said it was tough, but worth it because he helped to free Europe from fascism. I'm going to fight in Korea. This is my chance. My chance to make a difference like my brother did.

Joe: A chance for adventure. A chance to help out. I think our plans have just changed Mom. I know we were going to go on a trip to Montreal this summer, but I think that Murray and I will make a little side trip to Korea first.

The curtain closes, and ominous music plays.

SCENE 2: *THE REASONS WHY*

The Storytellers are animated and physically illustrate their words with descriptive movement.

Storyteller 2: What starts a war?

Storyteller 1: Let's say our whole world is like your playground. When you and another person have a disagreement, and your friends take sides, and line up behind the two with the first problem, it just gets bigger and bigger, and then gets out of control.

Storyteller 3: What was first a disagreement between two people becomes a fight between two gangs, and before you know it, the whole playground is involved! The First World War was like that. Both sides thought they would win in a few months. Instead, it took four terrible years.

Storyteller 1: …and the whole world was dragged into it.

Storyteller 2: The Korean War was something else. That was more like …. like your playground being divided in half down the middle with two different ways of playing on each side.

Storyteller 3: Only, after a while, the north side, who is playing with communist ideas and getting supplied with Soviet guns and Chinese soldiers, wants both sides to play together… THEIR way.

Storyteller 2: Meanwhile, the other half – the south side – who is playing with capitalist and democratic ideas is getting the help of Americans, isn't interested. But the North side won't take "No" for an answer, and decides to attack.

Storyteller 1: So the United Nations convinces you and other countries to join in and help South Korea keep their side of the playground.

Storyteller 3: And the Second World War?

Storyteller 1: Well, sometimes there really are bullies who have a high opinion of themselves. They think they're the best: they think, for no particular reason, that they're better than you, or you, or you! And they want to take over the playground to prove it!

Storyteller 2: This is called "fascism." Adolf Hitler, of Germany, was the biggest of the bullies in the European part of the world and Emperor Hirohito of Japan was the bully in the Asian part of the world.

Storyteller 3: First, others tried to make deals with those bullies: they let them get away with some bad things, hoping they wouldn't do other bad things.

Storyteller 1: In the end, they realized it wasn't going to work, that these bullies couldn't be trusted. It got to the point where the only way to stop them was to stand up to them. That's the way it is on the playground, and THAT's the way it was in the Second World War. Watch, and you'll see.

BULLY DANCE: *Dance and percussion piece "stomp style" about fascism. Both sides use a specific percussion instrument like; hockey sticks without the blades versus tin garbage can lids or large coffee tins.*

Dancers 1: *Wearing jeans and t-shirts of solid colours without labels or designs emerge in two lines from opposite sides of the stage. They build up a playful rhythm and end up facing each other. A leader does a "call and response" rhythm. The beat, movement and overall sounds are playful.*

Dancers 2: *Dressed entirely in dark shades emerge in a similar way from the two sides. Their beat is simple and menacing and steadily builds to overtake the sound of Dancers 1. Dancers 2 movements are stiff and soldier like and purposeful in a dark, deliberate manner. They encircle and overwhelm Dancers 1, forcing them to hand over their sticks. Dancers 1 shrink down and are hunched in the centre of the circle as Dancers 2 lord over them victoriously. Freeze as curtains close.*

SCENE 3: *THE WAR FRONT*

Storytellers step out of the curtain onto the apron of the centre stage.

Storyteller 1: Sometimes kids like to play at war. That's okay.

Storyteller 2: They like the bravery of being a hero.

Storyteller 3: They like the feeling of rightness when you're up against the bad guy.

Storyteller 1: They like to hide and spy, sneak up, and retreat.

Storyteller 2: They like the excitement of the game. And then, of course, they like to go home for their dinners at night.

Storyteller 1: If you were one of the men in our trio of wars,

Storyteller 2: If you were a member of their family,

Storyteller 3: You would know that in real life - it was not so easy.

Music is eerie. The curtain opens to reveal three tableaus: WWI soldiers sitting between sandbags; WWII soldiers resting against a backdrop of a destroyed building; the Korean War soldiers sitting on their knapsacks warming their hands over a propane stove or lantern. It's as if all three groups are taking a reflective break. At the end of the scene, they "jump to" and exit their positions.

WWI: *(sitting hunched between sandbags. The soldiers all participate in the conversation by talking directly to the audience.)*

George: Mud. That's what I'd say about this war. Mud. Ha! I used to love the feeling of it in the spring, between my toes. But now it's everywhere – in my food, between my fingers, in my hair and clogging up my boots.

Soldier 1: That's because this war got off to a strange start. We faced the enemy across the fields of France and Flanders, in Belgium. There weren't many trees, or the usual places to hide. So, we dug into the ground. Yeah, and then so did the enemy. And then we both dug deeper. They call this sopping mess "trenches," but we call it "home."

Soldier 2: When we fight, we go "over the top" and into a stinking mess of barbed wire, dead soldiers, and big craters from exploding shells sent long distances from artillery guns.

Soldier 1: Oh yes, and all that shelling makes for even more mud!

George: Another thing I'd say about this war is gas. Yes, gas. Not the kind that people laugh and joke about (*soldiers laugh*), or the kind you put into a motor coach to make it go, but the kind (*soldiers get very serious*) that floats across the fields on the wind like yellow death. The enemy surprised us the first time they used it, and the gas burned our lungs and many died, but we Canadians did not run.

Soldier 3: We did something ingenious and oddly surprising that day. I know a little about chemistry and I knew that uric acid neutralized gas, so-o-o-o-, we peed into our handkerchiefs and held them over our mouths and noses so we could breathe. You might laugh at the thought, but that's what saved many of us that day. Now they've issued us proper gas masks. Even then, when the gas alarms go off or you see the yellow mustard gas floating towards us, you have to act fast, or your lungs are finished.

George: So far our major battles have been the on the Somme, at Ypres, and our stunning victory at Vimy Ridge (*the other soldiers cheer*). And now its Passchendaele Ridge, the muddiest and most blasted place on the whole of the western front. It's almost time to go over the top again. Actually, what time is it? (*brings out watch and kisses it*) Hah! It's still ticking, and so am I.

Soldiers prepare to go over the top. Freeze. WWII soldiers come to life.

WWII: *Soldiers appear to be sharing a baguette on a break, leaning against a shattered brick wall, and eating small pieces that "Father" rips and passes out.*

Soldier 4: *(youngish and energetic)* We've got the Nazi's on the run! Finally! Finally this war is about covering ground and rooting out the enemy!

Soldier 5: *(older, and more seasoned)* Look at what we had to go through today to get here.

Soldier 4: UN-BE-LIEVABLE. I'll never forget that view from the ship's deck as we were going in! The sky a mass of bombers and fighters, the sea full of ships and boats of every description and the ships full of men, tanks, canons, supplies – and us!

Father: Funny, all I remember is the green faces of the sea sick guys around me. And then noise: the noise of thousands of bombers and fighters and naval guns blasting away. Simply indescribable. I thought I'd never live to hear my little girl sing again.

Soldier 6: *(realist)* Well we're on the ground now. This has gotta be the greatest invasion in the history of the world!

Soldier 4: *(expansively, blowing kisses to the wind)* Victory, here we come!

Soldier 5: Jacques, save the kissing for your girlfriend when you finally get home.

Father: I'll tell you something: this is my second time on the beaches of France. In 1942, I was with the Royal Regiment of Canada when we landed at Dieppe. What a disaster! Of us 5,000 Canadians who landed that day, 3,000 haven't been heard of – killed or captured. And I was one of the lucky ones. Today was my lucky day again. We took Juno Beach and I'm still alive – again.

Soldier 6: We're all lucky to have survived today.

Soldier 5: What made me join up was what happened to my cousin in Hong Kong. My cousin... like a brother to me.

Soldier 4: Yeah, right... *(remembering)* that was even before Dieppe.... go on....

Soldier 5: In Hong Kong, the Allies sent Canadian troops to help fortify the island against an expected Japanese attack. But they didn't send nearly enough. And when the Japanese invaded, they over-ran the island in no time. Don't know what happened to my buddies in the Winnipeg Grenadiers, but they and the people of Hong Kong are probably suffering terribly.

Soldier 4: I was jealous when the 1st Canadian Armoured Brigade and the Infantry Division shipped out to Sicily and Italy. Jealous of their chance to get on the ground and put two years of waiting behind them. I too wanted to take Italy back olive grove by olive grove, even if it meant I'd be crawling through the ruins.

Father: Well little buddy, you've got plenty of chances now. You won't be eating pasta in Italy, but hopefully you'll get to see tulips in Holland. Those Nazi's probably know they're going to lose, but you can be sure they still won't give up. We'll have to fight for every inch of territory through France, Belgium, and Holland.

Soldier 4: And we're going to bring those fascists down!

(Everyone nods and murmurs their agreement.)

Soldier 6: Shhh, what's that sound?

Soldiers stealthily pick up their guns and prepare for the unknown. Freeze. Korean War soldiers come to life. They start rubbing their hands over a Coleman stove can.

Korean War:

Joe: Cold! This war in Korea is cold! All I knew about Korea when I signed up was something about cherry blossom trees. And when I arrived, I find out there's no cherry blossoms because – it's winter! It's so cold I could have brought my hockey skates!

Murray: And what about them mountains! Who knew Korea had mountains – and plenty of them.

Soldier 9: When they told me I had to carry my Bren gun, which weighs almost as much as me, and my gear up and down those mountains, I thought they must be joking!

Soldier 7: When I signed up I was living in a small town that I used to call *Nowheresville*. Well, call me stupid, but *Nowheresville* looks pretty good to me right now!

Soldier 8: It's probably the same for the Chinese soldiers fighting with the North Koreans. They're sort of like you, buddy. One day they're village boys. And then something big happens in the world. Next thing they know, they're running up mountains in Korea with Canadians shooting at them.

Joe: At least we've done our very best for the South Koreans.

Murray: Our biggest victory was back in April, 1951, in the hills around Kap'yong.

Soldier 8: Did you know there were 8,000 enemy troops against us? That's eight of them for every one of us! But we held-out and won. The way Korean's tell it, the battle of Kap'yong stopped the communist forces from capturing their capital of Seoul.

Joe: Even my sister wrote to me to tell me that the newspapers called it "Canuck Heroism." My mother didn't want me to go to war in Korea, but after that she sure was proud.

Soldier 8: Well then Joe, since you seem so keen on making your mother proud of you, let's saddle up and get a move on. There'll be plenty more opportunities for you to make her proud before we're done here.

Eerie music. Curtains start to close as all three groups of soldiers leave the performance space and head out "on patrol" by staying low, slipping off the stage and dispersing through the audience and out the available doors.

Scene 4: The War Front in Korea

SCENE 4: *THE HOME FRONT*

CHOIR: *enters stage in front of closed curtain, and sings, "Till the Boy's Come Home (Keep the Home Fires Burning)" by Lena Guilbert Ford and Ivor Novello*

Storyteller 2: (*who has been singing with the choir*) What do you do when your son is far away in a dangerous place?

Storyteller 1: Or you miss your brother's teasing?

Storyteller 2: Or you can't get your Dad to help you with homework...for five years?

Storyteller 1: Sometimes you cry. A lot of times you're sad. But do you stop?

Storyteller 2: Do you give up?

Together: NEVER! You join the home front!

Curtains open

WWI: *Maman is knitting. She has a big basket of socks beside her rocking chair. Bettina is now a nurse in France and is wrapping bandages. Mathilde, dressed in overalls as a "farmerette," is hoeing in a garden.*

WWII: *Mother and the Factory Girls are dressed like "Rosie the Riveter" and wearing Munitions factory smocks. They stand in rows ready to set the factory line in motion. The children are sitting in front of them slightly off to the side, wrapping more layers on two large balls of tinfoil.*

Korean War: *Mom is wearing glasses and is sitting at a small desk, writing. She has a stack of newspapers beside her.*

WWI:

Maman: I am in a constant state of worry about George. The only thing that keeps my nerves in check is when I am knitting for the boys in the trenches. They say their feet are in a terrible state after being wet for days on end. They say they get a condition, called trench foot, and some of their toes actually turn black and rot off! Imagine that! So, besides cooking, cleaning, and my household chores, I spend every spare minute knitting. That or writing to George or Bettina.

Bettina: You won't find me at home with Maman anymore. George and most of our school chums are off fighting the war, and so I thought – why not me too? Why shouldn't I do my bit? That's when I decided to become a nurse. Here at the hospital we do whatever is necessary, even assist the doctors during surgery. But it is us who care for the boys afterwards. And so many times, you hear them call out for the ones they love. Especially their mothers. Just like when you go to bed, and you want your mother at your side, you hear these poor chaps at night calling out for the mothers, so far away.

Mathilde: I was too young to become a nurse or to work in a munitions factory worker, but I did the next best thing: I joined up to help bring in the harvest! With so many of our men away at the front there are only a few left to work the farms and gather the harvest. I get to wear trousers and bring in the wheat. Yup, farmerettes! That's what they call us! Look (*showing off her muscles*), wouldn't my brother George be surprised to see my new found muscles? I only pray he gets the chance.

Freeze.

Scene 4: The Home Front, WWI

WWII:

Hannah: Look, (*holding her tinfoil ball to the light*) I'm sure my ball is bigger than yours!

Jack: No way, I have about a million gum wrappers in this thing.

Hannah: But I got all the cigarette wrappers from Mom's work. Here, feel it, it's heavier than yours by far!

Jack: It doesn't really matter. What matters is that we are doing our very best to collect tin and other materials for the war effort.

Hannah: You're right Jack, every little bit counts. (*pulling bits of tin from her pocket*) Here, let's do this together. Here's (*pulling out a pocket full of tin bits*) a bunch more. I got them from the movie theatre.

Jack: At this rate we're going to have the biggest scrap metal ball in the history of our neighbourhood. And then we're going to hand it over to the factory, so's they can use it to make more tanks or whatever. Anything to help bring Dad home sooner.

Mother – in two lines with the Factory Girls – starts up the factory motions. Group does about 10 one-two movements with their arms. The factory line pauses "Break Time!" so each worker has a chance to step forward and speak.

Mother: (*longingly*) Working in this munitions factory on the afternoon shift, I really miss the kids. I get them up at six in the morning even though they don't have to leave for school until 8:30, just so that I can have the pleasure of their company. I check their homework and make them a good breakfast. I save the latest letters from my husband to read to them then…and we often write back right away. I miss the kids: but I really miss Eric too, and I can't help but feel my work here will bring him home faster.

Factory Girl 1: (*passionately*) Impatient? I'm the most impatient girl you ever met. And I can work fast enough for three! That's because I'm mad about the war, and all the fellas fighting overseas. In fact, tomorrow I'm joining the army myself. The Canadian Women's Army Corps! And when I get over there, I'll give the enemy a piece of my mind. (*Pulls out mirror from pocket, and spends time fixing hair and putting on makeup.*)

Factory Girl 2: (*dreamily*) They always said I was too dreamy to work in a factory. But what they don't know is that it's perfect for me: when your hands know what they have to do, your mind can drift away! Sometimes, I find myself thinking about how my mother, Nelda Delorme, survived her own stint in a munitions factory. It was in English speaking Massachusetts of all places! Then, she almost died after the Great War when she caught the Spanish influenza from my uncle, a returning soldier. I heard that more people died world-wide from the Spanish Flu than all the millions killed in the war! Mon Dieu! If she had died I wouldn't be here today doing the same thing – working in a munitions factory waiting for my husband to return, dreaming of our future babies...I'll name them all with D for my mother Delorme..Danielle, Denis...(*sigh*) In the meantime, here I am, drifting between the past and the future, while my hands are busy making munitions in the present. Crazy! (*holds them up as if to prove it and shakes head wonderingly*)

Factory Girl 3: (*defiantly*) As soon as the lads were called up for the fight, the government started making plans to put us girls to work in the factories. Like so many single girls I needed to work in order to help put food on my family's table. But do you think I could get a half-decent job? No! They said that the good jobs go to the men first because they had to feed their families. Like I don't need to? But now that I'm working in a good job with good wages, I don't plan on giving it up anytime soon. And just let them try and take it away from me! They'll see.

Factory Girl 4: (*worried*) We used to always receive letters from my cousin Rachel from Warsaw at the beginning of each month. They would come with their special stamps and mother would keep them for me to open. I would laugh my head off at all the tricks she would play on her brother David. But since the war started, her letters began to sound much more serious and I could tell there was something wrong. And then she stopped writing. I'm worried about her. Do you think something bad has happened? If I could, I would send her a ticket and money to come to Canada, if I only knew where she was.

Factory Girl 5: (*enthusiastically*) I love this job. And I love the girls I work with. It's funny that we call each other girls even though some of us are mothers and grandmothers. It's a hard job, but I love the feeling of camaraderie and friendship that exists between us, even though we come from many different walks of life. I also love having my own pay cheque with my name, "Rita", printed right on it. But I hate this war.

Factory Girl 2: (*calls out*) Break Time's over! Come on Ladies let's get back to work!

(*Group starts the actions again for about 10 one-two swings before freezing to indicate the end of the scene.*)

Scene 4: The Home Front, WWII

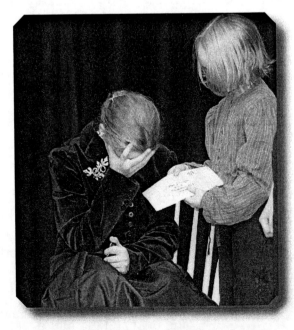

"Some of the men didn't come back"

Korean War:

Mom is writing at desk.

Mom: I'm writing letters to the newspapers. To complain and to remind them that they have a duty to ensure that the Korean War doesn't fade from the public's eye. The war is still raging over there, but if you ask me you wouldn't know it from reading the newspapers – unless of course you go to the back pages, where they seem to want to keep it out of sight. You see, my boy is in Korea. The government asked him to join up in the fight to keep communism from spreading into South Korea and the rest of the world, and he did. He left his family and his country to go and fight for Canada, and yet all we hear about is other places and other events. It's not right. It may not be much what I am doing, but the way I look at it, the more they shine a light on what is happening over there, the quicker it will be over. (*Drops head down to write more*)

Tina: (*rushing in with a newspaper*) Mom! It's over! The war in Korea is over! Take a look at this headline, fresh off the press! Headline: Korean Armistice Declared. Date: July 27, 1953. Location: Panmunjom, Korea. After two years, two weeks, and three days since the two sides began peace negotiations, the UN and Communist delegations have signed an armistice to end the fighting. It says that once the cease fire took effect both sides just shot off their left-over ammunition like crazy. Soldiers said it looked like the fireworks at the Canadian National Exhibition. They said a sea of Chinese soldiers stood across the valley, waving flags and shouting…. Well, I guess they must be just as glad as our boys to go home.

All three tableaus now unfreeze and continue their motions in a calm, steady manner. When the "soldiers" return to each of the tableaus, they slow down and freeze again. Movement is all in slow motion.

Storytellers: When peace came, when treaties were signed, when hostilities ceased, some of the men came back. (*Korean war soldier comes from the side and knocks at the door. Mother reaches to hold his hands.*)

Some men came back wounded. (*Father with crutches and arm wrapped in bandages enters across the centre back of the stage. Children see him first. "Daddy!" they call. Mother reaches to greet him.*)

And some men didn't come back at all. (*Deliveryman soldier walks in front of the stage. When he arrives, he knocks at the door. Mathilde answers. He takes his hat off his head and rests a moment with it on his heart. They look at each other. Then he pulls an envelope out of his bag and hands it to her. She passes it to Maman who motions for Mathilde to open it. She does. Mathilde slowly draws out the pocket-watch and holds it up high.*)

Mathilde: It's broken. (*Maman and Bettina put their head down in a tableau of grief.*)

Storytellers: BUT PEACE HAD COME. It was a gift they gave us – and it was earned with their youth, their talents, their time, and sometimes even their lives.

Curtains close.

CHOIR: *"Une Colombe"* by Celine Dion

SCENE 5: *CEREMONY OF REMEMBRANCE*

Curtains open onto the stage set with a Commonwealth War Graves Commission style headstone. The actors stand evenly spaced, two on one side and two on the other across the front of the stage. **See Teacher's Guide: Ceremony of Remembrance for additional details and procedures.**

Storyteller 1: It is said that time doesn't stand still for anyone. But don't you believe it. Time always stops for us on November 11, when we reflect on the gift of peace.

Storyteller 2: What does the gift of peace feel like to you? Is it gentle… soft, like when you drift off to sleep? Peace can be a quiet place of comfort within you.

Storyteller 3: But peace is more active than that.

Actor: Peace looks for the good in others.

Storyteller 1: It welcomes the stranger and those different from you.

Storyteller 2: It shouts joyfully, "Don't stand by yourself, JOIN US!"

Storyteller 3: Peace asks, "Would you like to play?" It notices, "Hey, you're different, I like that!"

Actor: Peace can also be serious. Sometimes it says, "I'm sorry, I'll try again", or "I don't understand, but explain it to me. I'm listening."

Storyteller 1: Peace is knowing how to live with what you need, and not be greedy for what you want. Peace respects and uses the shared resources of our world wisely.

Storyteller 2: Peace is full of grace. Especially when it sounds like "Thank you."

Storyteller 3: And so we say thank you to the men and women across the many generations whose sacrifices in times of war and peacekeeping helped to make us who we are today.

Storyteller 3: We say thank you to those who responded to the call of their leaders and fought valiantly and selflessly.

Storyteller 2: We say thank you to those cut down in the promise of their youth and the richness of their middle years.

Storyteller 3: We say thank you to those who paid the terrible cost of war. Let us use that knowledge to guide us towards peace.

Storyteller 1: We say thank you to all those Canadians who went before, whose contribution to the cause of freedom through two World Wars, the Korean War, and several United Nations Peacekeeping and UN sanctioned NATO missions forged a direction for our country and the world today.

Together: Together we remember. And we thank you.

The Honour March takes place to music which is solemn but moving, like "Hymn to the Fallen" from the movie "Saving Private Ryan."

Once the wreathe is laid that same person asks the audience to:

"PLEASE STAND"

- **BUGLE CALL: The Last Post**

- **MOMENT OF SILENCE**

- **The moment of Silence is ended when the wreathe-layer says, "Please join us in the singing of 'O Canada'."**

- **All sing "O Canada."**

Curtains close. The performance and Ceremony of Remembrance is ended.

**WWI Scenes at the Sunset Ceremony, Vigil 1914-1918 Project,
National War Memorial, November 10, 2008**

FOUR QUESTIONS ABOUT PEACE

A Play and A Ceremony

Suitable for Performance By: Grades 4 and up

Plot Summary:

The play opens with two student narrators observing the signs of November. "As soon as November begins there are certain things you can expect to see. Like bright red poppies on dark coats, old war movies on TV, grey skies and bare trees that seem to match the stories your grandparents tell you. It makes you think a lot. It makes you wonder. And questions just kind of POP into your head!" With that, four dancers, dressed in question marks, pop out of the audience to a light hearted yet thought provoking instrumental music piece. The ballet-style Dance of the Four Questions is the visual representation of the Narrator's deliberations. These four questions provide a framework for the scenes which follow. At the same time the questions are imaginatively answered through improvisation-style dramatizations or dramatic re-enactments.

Scene 1: What does "peace" really mean?

Three basic peaceful scenes are explored – in the family, in the playground, in society – each of which ends in the opposite of peace. For example, apparent family harmony evolves into a series of disagreements which concludes when the parent finally yells, "Can't we have any peace and quiet around here!"

Scene 2: How did our peacekeeper reputation begin?

Lester B. Pearson steps on stage to recount how his earlier experiences in WWI and WWII lead him to work for peace. The crisis over the Suez Canal, where he effectively halts diplomats from Israel, France, and Britain from going to war with Egypt's Colonel Nasser, is re-enacted.

Scene 3: Where do Canadians keep the peace?

Soldiers are seen performing a variety of peacekeeping, and peacemaking duties in six vignettes which take place all over the world. These include Cyprus (1992), Golan Heights (1991), Namibia (1990), and the Balkans (1991). As well, Globe and mail reporter Christie Blatchford makes an appearance when she interviews soldiers involved in de-mining activities in Afghanistan in 2006.

Scene 4: How can we make peace in our world?

The actors in Scene 1 reappear and explore each of the scenarios – in the home, on the playground, in society – in a concretete context related to students' lives. In this way they provide relevant answers that promote Canadian values and world peace.

Acting Roles:

Speaking roles: 46 individual roles
2 non-speaking (stretcher bearers)

Group scenes for additional non-speaking roles:

- protest scenario

Music/Choral Options:

There are possibilities for choral pieces or musical interludes between each scene. (See list of possibilities in Teacher's Guide: Staging) The contemporary nature of this play lends itself nicely to soliciting music ideas from the students, or having them chose from a selection, the songs they think fit best.

Dance Options:

Dance of the Four Questions: Dancers whose clothing are adorned with question marks, rise out of the audience to light hearted yet thought provoking instrumental music. An accompaniment of bells or chimes would also be effective.

Characters and Costumes

In order of appearance. Roles with full names are based on real people.
Use the character list below to record the names of your cast members.

SCENE 1: *WHAT DOES PEACE REALLY MEAN?*

Narrator 1 and 2: (*vivacious, confident performers who walk directly to the audience. The Narrators are the guides who lead us on this exploration of "peace." They can be imaginatively blocked and can remain on stage, offside or sit among the choir or audience in between their performance moments. It is, in some sense, as if they are seeing their thoughts come alive.*)

Scenario Groups:

Family: Mom, Dad, Grandparents, Children (3)

Playground: Chanters (3), New Kid (1), Ball Players (2). Teeter-totters (2)

Community Protest Scene: Protesters, Police Officers (2) Bystanders (2)

There are two options to play this scene:

1. With an "improv style" group in which one scenario transforms into another and props are mimed. In that case, actors could wear blue jeans and one coloured t-shirts without labels.

2. In the case of three distinct scenario groups, actors can dress appropriately for their role in the family, playground or protest scene.

Scene 2: *How did our peacekeeper reputation begin?*

Lester B. Pearson: *(1950's suit, bow tie)*

Secretary: *(pearls and secretary's suit)*

Two Stretcher Bearers: *(WWI boots and leggings, wool army jacket)*

Flight Instructor: *(dashing WWI flight instructor)*

Britain: *(diplomat's outfit, sign around neck with name of country)*

France: *(diplomat's outfit, sign around neck with name of country)*

Israel: *(diplomat's outfit, sign around neck with name of country)*

President Colonel Nasser (Egypt): *(dressed as Nasser)*

Scene 3: *Where do Canadians help to keep peace?*

Soldiers are dressed in a variety of army gear using or miming props depending on the climate of the location they are stationed, as well as the task they are involved in.

Cyprus 1999

Cypress Soldier 1: _____

Cypress Soldier 2: _____

Cypress Soldier 3: _____

Cypress Soldier 4: _____

Golan Heights, Israel, 1991

Golan Heights Soldier 1: _____

Golan Heights Soldier 2: _____

Golan Heights Soldier 3: _____

Namibia, 1990

Soldier Dad: _____

Elise (*youngish daughter*): _____

Nicaragua, 1990

Nicaraguan Soldier 1: _____

Nicaraguan Soldier 2: _____

Nicaraguan Soldier 3: _____

Nicaraguan Soldier 4: _____

Balkans 1991

Balkan Soldier 1: _____

Balkan Soldier 2: _____

Balkan Soldier 3: _____

Balkan Soldier 4: _____

Afghanistan, 2006

Afghanistan Soldier 1: _____

Afghanistan Soldier 2: _____

Afghanistan Soldier 3: _____

Christine Blatchford: *(reporter, dressed in fatigues, carrying recorder and note pad)*

Scene 4: How can we make peace in our world?
Same actors as Scene 1

Scene 5: A Ceremony of Remembrance

Scene 1: *What does "peace" really mean?*

As the audience enters the auditorium/gym, current popular music about war and peace could be playing while images of Canadian peacekeepers and their efforts could be projected on a screen.

Choir: *Any song that reflects about peace.*

Narrator 1: When November comes around again each year, there are certain things you can expect to see. Like bright red poppies on dark coats... Are YOU wearing one?

Narrator 2: I look forward to watching old war movies on TV. The skies are grey and the trees are bare. The night's are cold. Everything seems to match the stories your grandparents tell you about the olden days.

Narrator 1: It makes me think of things.

Narrator 2: It makes me wonder.

Narrator 1: And questions just kind of...POP into your head and stay swirling about!

Dance of the Four Questions: A ballet-style modern dance allows the dancers to visually represents the Narrator's questions. When the word POP is spoken, the four questions POP up from the audience and swirl to the front. Their dance costumes are covered with questions. There can be a small dance sequence to a short piece of instrumental music. The tone could be light hearted yet thought provoking. An accompaniment of bells or chimes would also be effective.

ISBN: 9781554950683

Narrator 2: In November, we hear a lot of talk about war.

Narrator 1: And a lot of talk about peace.

Narrator 2: You must hear these words too. War and Peace. Peace, of course, means the opposite of war. It also makes me think of one of my favourite ways of being; a nice, calm, kind of quiet way to be.

Narrator 1: But what does the word "peace" really mean? Let's think about that for a few moments and check out some of the places in our lives where we can expect to find peace, starting with this family.

Three staging possibilities exist:

1. *The improv-style performance where the actors transform from one group into the next using mimed props*
2. *The three distinct scenario groups where the curtain opens to reveal all of them frozen in tableau on the stage*
3. *The three distinct scenario groups which take place in three different locations in the performance space; on the stage, in front of the stage, or entering the side doors.*

<u>**Family Scene:**</u> *Parents contentedly making a meal in the kitchen, grandparent sitting on the chair reading the newspaper, kids (two) watching TV, while a third sibling studies. Block it so there is movement across the tableau. Pleasant conversation for a few moments follows.*

Parent: Do you need any help?

Child 3: (*studying*) Not right now Dad, but thanks for asking.

Parent: So how was your piano lesson?

TV Watching Children: Good. And we finished our homework too.

Parent: (*to grandparent*) What did the repair man say about our furnace today Grandpa?

Grandparent: He said it only needed a little adjustment, and he fixed it in five minutes.

Parent: Thank goodness for that! I thought we'd get hit with a big bill!

Parent: Any hockey practices tonight?

TV Watching Children: No

Parent: Great. I just love it when we're all home together? It's so peaceful!

(*Tableau freezes. Family members can add to the "check" with their own way of saying it, for example using phrases like "Yes! You bet! Of course!"*)

Narrator: Have you got the basic things you need to stay alive? For example, have you got a place to live?

Grandparent: Check

Narrator: Have you got nutritious food?

Mother: Check

Narrator: Do you have clean water to drink?

Father: Check

Narrator: Have you got medical help when you're sick or injured?

Child: Check

Narrator: Do you go to school?

Child: Check

Narrator: Do you have most of the things, and even some of the things you don't need but want?

Adult: Check

Narrator: Then you've got peace.

Conversation continues but this time conflicts evolve.

Parent 1: By the way, did you remember to pick up my stuff from the dry-cleaners?

Parent 2: No, sorry, I forgot.

Parent 1: No wonder you forgot. You're so wrapped up in your own affairs you forget to think of anyone else.

Parent 2: Yes, I *am* busy at work. And I'll tell you something else, I had a look at our bank statement and I see you've been buying new sports equipment for yourself again.

Parent 1: Yeah, so? I need new running shoes (*or hockey skates*).

Parent 2: New running shoes? Since when have your feet been growing? Didn't you buy yourself a new pair of shoes just last month?

(*Freeze*)

Child 1: Hey, I don't want to watch that show!

Child 2: You got to choose last time. It's my turn.

Child 1: You always choose the lamest stuff.

Grandparent: Turn down that TV. It's always so LOUD. I can't hear myself think!

Child 3: (*noticing the TV watching sibling*) Hey, that's my favourite t-shirt you're wearing.

Child 2: So what, you always take my ipod without asking.

Parents: STOP! Can't we get any PEACE and QUIET around here!

(*Tableau freezes. Curtains close.*)

Narrator: OOPS!

(*Loud recess bell rings.*)

Playground Scene: (*The children are in a playground at the start of recess.*)

Chanters: (*Run holding hands. Then launch into chanting with motions.*)

> Girl friend, girl friend, dressed in blue,
> These are the motions you must do:
> Stand at attention: stand at ease,
> Bend your elbows: bend your knees.
> Salute to the captain, bow to the queen;
> Turn your back on the dirty submarine.
> I can do the heel-toe; I can do the splits.
> I can do the wiggle-waggle just like this!
> (*All wiggle-waggle and freeze.*)

Ball Player 1: Hey! Aren't you the new kid in class.

New Kid: Yeah.

Ball Player 2: What are you staring at?

New Kid: Just the school year. It's so nice here – there's a play structure, and a sandbox and plenty of room to play basketball and soccer. My last school had a dirt yard and only older boys could use the basketball hoop.

Balla Player 2: Do you want to play with us?

New Kid: Sure!

Ball Player 1: Here, catch!

(Gets ready to throw it/catch it. Freeze.)

Teeter-totter: *(Each one shouts as they get to the "top" of the teeter-totter.)*

> I LO-O-O-O-O-V-V-E Recess!
> No school work!
> No home chores!
> No multiplication tables!
> No clean your room!

Together: ONLY PLAY TIME!

(Tableau freezes. Playground members can add to the "check" with their own way of saying "Yes! You bet! Of Course")

Narrator 1: Do you have a lot of friends?

Chanters: Check

Narrator 2: When you're done with your chores and finished your homework, do you get to play?

Teeter-Totter: Check

Narrator 2: Do you have a place where it's safe to play, a place with no bombs or land mines or toxic pollution?

New Kid: Check

Narrator 1: And in that place, can you be yourself, without teasing or bullying?

Chanters: Check

Narrator 2: Then you've got peace.

(Conversation and action begin again. Tension and discord build in the playground.)

Ball Player 1: You want the ball?... here, you can have it! *(throws it with unnecessary force)*

New Kid: *(after getting whacked)* Owwww! What did you do that for?

Ball Player 1: It's just something we do to new kids around here.

(Freeze)

Chanters: Salute to the captain, bow to the queen;
Turn your back on the dirty submarine.
I can do the heel-toe; I can do the splits.
I can do the wiggle-waggle just like this!
(*All three wiggle-waggle.*)

Teeter-Totters: (*Gesturing at the Chanters*) Look at them! They look so stupid!

Ball Players: Hey! What's that? (*They start imitating the "wiggle waggle."*)
You gotta be kidding!
You guys look crazy!
Nahhhh, they must Be crazy!

(*At the same time a teeter-totter kid gets a hold of the ball and also whacks it at the New Kid.*)

New Kid: What did you do that for?

Teeter-Totters: Aren't you listening? It's what we do to new kids we don't like.

Chanters: (*offended and upset*) Quit making fun of us! Leave us alone and let us play in peace!
(*turn inward to group and huddle together. Freeze*)

Narrators: OOPS!

Community Protest Scene:
(*It's a peaceful protest. The issue here is "Water legislation and conversation," but feel free to insert a local current issue instead. Protesters are carrying signs like Water is too precious for politics; Don't sell our water!; The North Pole is melting. Do you care?) They are walking in a circular motion and are calling out a pro-environment chant. A few are handing out pamphlets to those walking by.*

Protester: What do we need?

Group: Change!
When do we need it?
Now!
What do we need?
Water protection!
When do we need it?
Now!
What do we need?
Change!
When do we need it?
Now!

Bystander 1: What's going on officer?

Police Officer: It's just a little demonstration Miss.

Bystander 2: What the heck are they protesting about?

Police Officer: They want the government to change the laws protecting Canadian waters from pollution or being sold-off.

Bystander 2: That's a joke! Don't we live beside one of the biggest fresh water lakes in the world?

Bystander 1: Well, yes we do, but there's been a lot of chemicals and other pollutants dumped into those lakes for years.

Bystander 2: Listen, my generation needs jobs more than we need a bunch of crybabies complaining about water – we've got to start using our natural resources to create more jobs and stop worrying about water.

Protester: Hi there. We're here today hoping to educate people about some very serious issues concerning our use of fresh water. Please have a look at this. (*hands a pamphlet*)

Bystander 1: Oh, yes, thank you very much, I....I'll have a look at it.

(*Tableau freezes. Community members can add to the "check" with their own way of saying Yes! You bet! Of course!*)

Narrator 1: Do you follow the rules? Do you live up to the responsibilities we have as citizens?

Police, Protestors, Bystanders: Check

Narrator 2: Can you live the way that best suits your beliefs without interfering with how other people choose to live their lives?

Police, Protestors, Bystanders: Check

Narrator 1: Can you freely voice your opinion?

Protesters: Check

Narrator 2: When you think something is wrong or unfair, can you speak your mind without fear of being hurt or humiliated?

Police, Protesters, Bystanders: Check

Narrators: Then you have peace.

(*Conversation begins and discord builds*)

Bystander 2: Educating the public? You mean harassing the public! What gives you the right to stand here spreading a bunch of lies, and then say you're doing me a favour? A water crisis? There is no water crisis!

Protester: Sir, I think that maybe if you just take a look at this... (*tries to hand over pamphlet but Bystander 2 whacks it away*)

Bystander 2: (*to Police Officer*) They're harassing me! You hear me officer! This is a public sidewalk and they are harassing me!

Police: Well, actually in Canada people have the right to protest and ...

Bystander 2: A bunch of no-good, tree-hugging rabble rousers. They're blocking my way on a public street! Is this what I pay my taxes for?

Police: Well, well... okay (*to the protestors*) Come on now, you can't block the sidewalk, you have to let people pass. Now please move along.

Protestors: What do you mean move along?
There's plenty of room! We've got the right to protest!
We haven't taken over the sidewalk!

(*The police start to coral the protestors, indicating they should move along. The scene ends with someone shouting.*)

Bystander 2: Yah, get lost! Take your nonsense somewhere else! We prefer to keep the peace here! (*Protestors are pushed off the stage by the Police and the Bystanders move arrogantly by.*)

Narrators: OOPS! (*Curtains close.*)

Musical Interlude: (*Your choice.*)

SCENE 2: *HOW DID OUR PEACEKEEPER REPUTATION BEGIN?*

Narrator: (*wonderingly*) Well, I guess that peace means different things to different people. I thought peace was that gentle feeling of calm that we call peacefulness. Is peace more than that? (*pauses and paces*)

Narrator 2: Yes, it is. Peace is more than just feeling calm and settled – it has to do with choices we make and how we act. In our lives we have to make choices. Sometimes people make bad choices or do wrong things. They might think they are doing "the right thing" – but in fact, it's only the right thing for them. That doesn't mean you end up with world wars breaking out. But sometimes in our families, on our playgrounds and in our communities, people make choices that lead to something that looks like war.

Narrator 1: So .... (*slowly and deliberately*) peace is about the choices we make and how we act in the world.

Narrator 2: That's right. You have to choose to be a kind and peaceful person, and a country has to choose to be a caring and peaceful country.

Narrator 1: How is it then that Canada made the choice to become a leader amongst peacekeeping nations?

Pearson: (*steps out of the curtains*) Actually, I'd be happy to answer that question for you.

Narrator 2: Why, its Prime Minister Lester B. Pearson, the father of peacekeeping. We'd be honoured to hear from you Sir!

Pearson: Certainly. My pleasure. I always enjoyed a walk down memory lane. My idea of international peacekeeping started in World War One. (*Curtain opens to reveal a stool he sits on, and a bench piled with the three stacked volumes of his memoirs, his pipe, and a WWI helmet.*)

Have you ever had a birthday wish? (*laughs heartily*) Of course you have. Well my birthday wish when I turned 18 was to head out for an adventure. It just so happened that when I turned 18 the First World War had just begun, and what better adventure could a young man of my generation hope for than to join an army that was headed off to war. So on April 23, 1915, I enlisted as Private Pearson, #1059 in the Canadian Army Medical Corps.

(*Curtains open fully to reveal two WWI stretcher bearers briskly crossing the back stage. Pearson quickly puts on the helmet and pulls on the Red Cross armband, going towards the stretcher. he checks the body for vital signs, shakes his head, and sadly watches as they go offstage. Walks back to the stool and takes off the armband.*)

After some time in the Medical Corps I decided it wasn't for me. I was a young man anxious to do something really exciting, so I joined the Royal Flying Corps. While in pilot training my instructor took me aside.

(*Flight instructor enters stage right. Pearson jumps to attention.*)

Flight Instructor: Lester? Lester Pearson? What kind of a name is that for a flying ace? You'd better change your name if you seriously plan on successfully targeting German flying aces. Let's see... Pierre Pearson? No.... Allan Pearson? No.... Mike...Mike....Mike Pearson. That's it! From now on your name is "Mike Pearson!"

Pearson: "Mike!" And it stuck. From then on I was Mike Pearson. (*he laughs*) But especially my friends call me Mike.

(*Stands up and moves forward as the curtains close. Becomes impassioned and convincing.*)

All joking aside, and to answer your questions, my experience in the First World War changed my view of what war was about. Like so many young men in my time, I had this romantic idea that going to war would be a patriotic adventure, a chance to do my bit for my country. But once I saw war and its aftermath I began to questions the deeper meaning of war. And so I asked myself the questions: "Why do countries or politicians choose the path of death and destruction to solve international problems? Isn't there a better way?" It was then I decided that I would devote my life to working as a diplomat for the betterment of my country and for lasting peace in the world.

After the war I was appointed by the Canadian government as a diplomat in London, England and in Washington.

(*Secretary enters with papers to sign.*)

Secretary: Excuse me Mr. Pearson, these papers have just arrived from Winston Churchill.

Pearson: Thank-you. I'll have a look at them now.

Secretary: (*in a confiding and complimentary manner*) Lester Pearson is an extraordinary diplomat. He works hard, he listens hard, and he understands even the most difficult problems. You could say he's, ahem, very diplomatic! On top of which, he is the most friendly fellow. Mr. Pearson appreciates that to be a successful diplomat everyone's opinion must be respected.

Pearson: In 1945, when the Second World War ended, I was Canada's Ambassador to the United States. As such, I was fortunate to have played an important role in establishing the United Nations and the North Atlantic Treaty organization, also known as NATO.

Secretary: Mr. Pearson was also President of the General Assembly of the United Nations, which is a kind of world government, at the time of the Korean War – another war that we remember Canadian service men and women for on Remembrance Day.

Pearson: After the Korean War, the next world crisis I was involved in was the Suez Canal, in 1956. The Suez Canal is a masterpiece of maritime engineering that crosses Egypt. It was opened in 1869 and links the Mediterranean Sea with the Indian Ocean. It allows ships to take a short cut across the middle east instead of going all the way around Africa to get to Asian countries. (*Secretary hands back all the papers and pen and then makes a flourish rolling out a long blue cloth over the edge of the stage.*)

Secretary: Didn't General Nasser take the canal away from the British and French company that built it... and then his government nationalized it, saying it belonged to the Egyptian people?

Pearson: Yes he did. And it was then that the trouble began.

(An angry crowd of "diplomats" come bursting through the gym/auditorium doors. They wave fists at each other and shout things like: "Well, I never!", "How dare YOU!", "It belongs to us – we developed it.", "It's our land." as befits their role. As they reach the stage, they separate on each side of the "blue canal:" Egypt on one side, and Israel, Britain and France on the other. This scene is delivered with a fair bit of posturing and aggrieved gestures.)

Colonel Nasser: I am President Colonel Nasser, and my great ambition is to work for Egypt's progress.

Israel: Progress? How can you say that seizing the Suez Canal is progress?

Nasser: I took control of the canal because it is part of my country and my country belongs to my people.

Britain: What about the foreign companies who paid a lot of money to build it? What about *their* investment.

Nasser: We'll pay them what it is worth, of course – a fair market value.

France: But how will our ships get through the canal?

Nasser: The same way as always – they'll float. *(France shakes head as if he doesn't believe it.)* Now the money made from the canal will go to the Egyptian people, instead of foreign companies. And this money we will use to build the Aswan Dam, to bring much needed electricity to my people.

Britain: This is not acceptable to Britain, to France or to Israel. If you don't back down, we will invade!

Nasser: *(bitterly)* Our minds are made up! The Suez Canal is ours!

France and Britain: The Americans will join us!

Nasser: If that is so, then the countries of the Middle East and the Soviet Union will join us against you!

All: And the world will be at war again, and it will be *(pointing)* YOUR FAULT!

(Pearson jumps down between them and physically separates them. They freeze in a tableau of aggressive stance towards each other. He then turns back to the audience.)

Pearson: Britain, France, and Israel invaded Egypt to take back the Suez Canada, but luckily for the world, the Americans and the Russians didn't get involved. At that time I was Canada's representative at the United Nations, and I suggested the UN should establish a United Nations Emergency Force made up of troops from around the world and send it to Egypt to keep the armies separated until they reached a peace settlement. The UN agreed. And it worked. This became known as "peacekeeping," although at the time there was really no peace to keep.

France, Britain, Israel, and Nasser: (*start thawing at "UN Emergency Force" and respond by becoming deep in consideration and murmuring*) An international force of soldiers from other countries .... they would be impartial ... we would never think of attacking them .... this would allow us to cool off a bit and ... save face ... and come to a peace settlement ... We Agree! (*They reach to shake hands with each other but then stop and instead shake hands with Pearson, who in turn transmits the handshake to the other. The diplomats walk off in a dignified manner.*)

Secretary: That's how the United Nations took on its role of peacekeeping. It was Mike Pearson's idea. And Canada's idea too. That's how Canada got its reputation as the world's foremost peacekeeping nation. For his efforts, Mr. Pearson was awarded the Nobel Peace Prize in 1957.

Pearson: It was said that I had kept the world safe from war. THAT is the prize which matters most to me. (*Smiles and quietly walks offstage.*)

Musical Interlude: Modern song that is the student's choice.

SCENE 3: *WHERE DO CANADIANS KEEP THE PEACE*

Narrator 2: And that's how Canada became a leader amongst peacekeeping nations: Mike Pearson – I mean the Right Honourable Prime Minister Lester B. Pearson – came up with the idea in 1956 for the United Nations, during the Suez Crisis. Did the United Nations choose to use peacekeeping again, and did Canada choose to participate?

Narrator 1: There's the word "choose" again. Yes, we did choose peacekeeping again. And many, many times after that. Canada has a well earned reputation for being one of the world's leading peacekeeping nations.

Cyprus (New Year's Eve, 1992)

Cypress 1: (*sarcastically, tiredly*) Well me boys, are you ready for another evening stroll on the lovely island of Cyprus?

Cypress 2: Pretty funny, Tony. Another evening stroll, when what you mean is an another evening patrol – along the Green Line. And what's so lovely about an island where the Greek Cypriots and the Turkish Cypriots would probably kill each other if we weren't here?

Cypress 3: Think about it. Over 25,000 Canadian troops have rotated in and out of Cypress since we first came here in 1964. So ... that's 29 years of Canadian peacekeepers in Cyprus. If every one of those troops patrolled 10 kilometres a day, that would make – let me see ... I don't know ... maybe a million kilometres of ... .

Cypress 1: Oh, come on Olivier, enough with math already. Here it is – New Year's Eve 1992 – and what I wouldn't give to be back in London tonight, with Erika and the kids. Instead I'm 10,000 kilometres away, lacing up my boots to go out in the rain again. And I can't even phone home to wish them a Happy New Year!

Cypress 3: Do you know that Cyprus is smaller than Cape Breton Island? That's where I'm from. You could walk clear across this island quicker than Pete if it weren't for the demilitarized zone keeping the two sides apart.

Cypress 3: I don't get it. They were all born here, on the same small island. Just on two different branches of the same family tree, if you know what I mean.

Cypress 1: My dad was <u>here</u> back in 1964, when the UN first asked us to keep the Turks and the Greeks apart. There was a lot of unrest then, but we did maintain a fragile peace. That is until their mother countries got involved. Greece wanted the island for themselves, and the Turks invaded from the other side.

Cypress 2 and 3: Then things got really hot!

Cypress 1: Hot is right! We barely managed to keep a lid on things. That's when the Green Line was established down the centre of the island. There were some deaths – Canadian peacekeepers too. But if we hadn't been here there would have been all out war between Greece and Turkey.

Cypress 3: You know I've had four tours of duty here since 1964.

Cypress 2: This is my second, and hard as it is, it's hardest on my family. My kid's hockey team has won the divisional championship a couple of times and I've never been there to see them do it.

Cypress 1: Well, you can forget about the Blue Line. It's the Green Line we've go to worry about.

Curtains close as they jump off stage and walk out of the auditorium greeting the audience as if the are "locals", e.g. "How are you tonight?"; "Cute baby! Is he walking yet?"

Golan Heights, Israel, with the UN Disengagement Observer Force (1991)

Golan 1 brings out a stool in front of curtain and perches on it while writing on a clipboard. Two other soldiers sneek up behind him and grab it and read it.

Golan 1: Hey Peter, what's this? I thought you were writing a letter to your wife?

Golan 2: The first thing I always do is write a letter to Anne. Then afterwards – if I feel like it – I write a little verse. it helps keep me sane, especially now we're worried that the Iraqi's might start using chemical weapons on Israel.

Golan 3: Verse? You're writing poetry about the Gulf War? Who ever heard of a peacekeeping poet? (*laughs*)

Golan 1: Yeah, and what's to say? The war is in Kuwait. All we do is sit here in these hilly observation posts in the Golan Heights just looking around. What's the point of that?

Golan 2: The point is to make sure that the Syrians and the Israelis don't send any troops into the area of separation between them. If they do, our job in the UN Disengagement Observer Force is to report it and to tell them to get out. We've been doing that since 1974. Listen to my poem – I think it says what we're here for.

When I am back home sometime later this year,
Some guy at the Legion will buy me a beer.
He'll ask what I did in the War in the Gulf.
This is the question I've been asking myself.

Golan 1: *If you read in the papers 'bout the troops in Bahrain,*
They'd have you believe that we missed the train.
Too far from the action to really be vets,
Just driving our trucks instead of fast jets.

Golan 3: *The "human interest," it seems, was at Canada Dry One,*
Where tensions were high 'neath the hot Arab sun.
So CBC news didn't get to the Heights,
To spend time in the shelters on SCUD-alert nights.

Golan 1: *The flames of the war didn't come very near.*
And maybe, just maybe, it's because we were here.
Just doing our jobs, day after day,
Unnoticed by most and for no danger pay.

Golan 2: *I guess in peacekeeping there isn't much glory.*
We didn't make the news as some feature story.
But we were here before those other guys came,
And I'll look at that guy who is buying me beer:
"Yes I did my part in that war in the east;
I was up in the Golan, just keeping the peace."

Golan 3: Not bad Pete, not bad at all. That pretty well sums it up if you ask me.

Golan 1: Come on. Let's get ourselves up to the observation post and do us some more "Keeping the peace." Hey Pete, (*voice becomes cajoling*) I'm trying to keep the peace at home. Think you would consider writing a poem that I could send home to my girlfriend?

(*Poem written by Officers serving with CCUNDOF-the Canadian Contingent of UNDOF. Published in the Camp Ziouani Monthly Review, March 1991, and in Granatstein, J.L. and Douglas Lavender. Shadows of War, Faces of Peace: Canada's Peacekeepers. Toronto: Key Porter Books, 1992.*)

Namibia, 1990

Soldier Dad sits on one side of the stage writing the letter, while his young daughter stands at the other side of the stage surrounded by some toys. Together they mime reading or writing the letter.

Soldier Dad: November 1990. Dear Elise,

Elise: Don't you just love the stamps on this envelope? Please don't forget to save them for your collection.

Soldier Dad: I am writing to you from northern Namibia, near the Angolan border. If you look at a map of Africa, I'm just about where it's bellybutton would be – if Africa had a belly button! I have driven 1,600 kilometres this last month, and I have already gone through 27 tires.

Elise: I know you are good at division, and maybe you could figure out how many kilometres each tire lasted, and let me know in your next letter. I was glad to hear you enjoyed your Brownie Camp. Did you tell them that your Dad camps out every night? Or that we sleep close to the fire to keep the snakes away? You should see the beetles here: they're as big as your fist and climb right over us when we are sleeping. I don't think your Brownies would want to do any camping around here!

Soldier Dad: I'm sorry I couldn't call you on your birthday, Elise. That day I had to drive two United Nations representatives from Ireland into the hills so they could observe the elections to make sure they're fair and square. This way the Namibian people will finally have the chance to elect an independent government.

Elise: You know, Elise you are learning so much about Namibia I'll bet you could earn your world politics badge from the Brownies just by reading my letters. I love and miss you very much. Your Dad, Bombardier Bernard Atkinson. P.S. I'll put my kiss right on this x.

After he makes a large "x" movement on his paper, the two, at the same time, slowly and deliberately lift the paper to their lips and kiss it with a loud "smack."

Central America: Nicaragua, 1990

Group sits two in front and two behind. They initially make the "doo-doo-doo-doo" sound of helicopter blades and gently sway in unison as one pilots the helicopter. When not speaking, they look out of the side windows with binoculars.

Nicaragua 1: Too bad our Canadian helicopters didn't arrive in time!

Nicaragua 2: No kidding. Last time we rented one of these local helicopters, I opened the window to let in some fresh air, and the whole darn clamshell door fell right off. Fell right into Lake Nicaragua! That was a lot more air than I bargained for!

Nicaragua 1: You're telling me.

Nicaragua 3: It certainly makes you appreciate Canadian mechanics and maintenance!

Nicaragua 4: Do you think this mission will be worth it?

Nicaragua 2: You better believe it. But it's a calculated risk – because we're here as observers and not soldiers with guns. But the idea is to get the opposing forces to put down their guns, to begin talking with each other and to start acting like decent human beings once again. To do that we'll use good offices, our military common sense and respect for the forces that are demobilizing.

Nicaragua 1: The only problem is that many of the soldiers on both sides don't know we're here or what we're doing.

Nicaragua 3: That's why it's important for us to get out there and get ourselves seen. Once they start to recognize our blue berets and the markings on our aircraft the sooner they'll stop taking pot-shots at us because they think we're the enemy. They will also recognize that the world is watching and is here to help.

Nicaragua 4: You're right. What a job ahead! We have to take a guerrilla army of 23,000 soldiers and get them to give up their weapons without fighting.

Nicaragua 1: Hey! Look down below! There's the Contra army!

Nicaragua 2: Thousands and thousands of them!

Nicaragua 3: Looks like they're having lunch for heaven's sake!

Nicaragua 4: And no one's firing on us! But, boy do they look surprised.

Nicaragua 1: Hey, look, they're waving!

Nicaragua 2: I guess they really ready for peace!

Curtains close

Balkans (Yugoslavia, 1990)

Soldiers on patrol slide up the centre of the isle to ominous music, then stop in front of curtained stage for a "break."

Balkans 3: This is a safe spot boys. Let's take a break.

Balkans 1: My wife tells our kids that I'm peacekeeping in the former Yugoslavia: but what I can't figure out, is how are we supposed to keep the peace when war is raging all around us?

Balkans 2: Who are we here for anyway Chris? You've got the highest rank so you should know. Is it for The Bosnians? The Croats? The Serbs?

Balkans 3: We are here for none of them, but all of them. We're supposed to keep them away from one another and to assist civilians caught up in the fighting.

Balkans 4: Whose lame brain scheme was this anyway?

Balkans 1: The European Union asked for UN assistance. The Balkans – which is what this part of the world is referred to – has always been a kind of tinder-box. One spark here back in 1914 is what touched off the First World War.

Balkans 2: So the nations of Europe don't like a war in their backyard and so they call on the United Nations to try and bring peace – in the middle of a war zone? That's more like peace*making* instead of peace*keeping*, isn't it?

Balkans 2: Exactly.

Balkans 3: I was down in the Medak Pocket when the Croation army attacked us Canadians. They fired hundreds of artillery shells at us and their troops attacked us. They thought we would high-tail it out of there and then they could continue their advance against the Serbs. What they didn't know was that the Princess Pats have never run from a fight. When they realized this they backed off and withdrew. That was the heaviest fighting Canadians have done since the Korean War, and frankly, my heaviest fighting *ever*.

Balkans 4: I know what you mean Chris. This is some dangerous place too. Yesterday I was in a village where the Serbs burned down a 500 year old mosque. I've seen the results of systematic looting and destruction of whole towns and villages from all sides. They even kill all the animals and throw their bodies down the wells to destroy the water supply.

Balkans 2: Now to mention the War Crimes. There's been massacres of civilians on all sides, and if we can help put a stop to that I guess we're here for a good reason. Nevertheless, this is one nasty and dirty war. I just hope we can make a difference.

Balkans 3: Okay boys, break's over. Saddle up and let's get going!

Soldiers slink carefully offstage.

Afghanistan, 2006

Curtains open. Soldiers (male and female) are involved in de-mining. They carefully move away from their spot and back off, laying down their equipment and stretching out their muscles. Christie Blatchford walks purposefully on stage.

Christie Blatchford: Hey guys, I'm Christie Blatchford, a journalist with the Globe and Mail. Thanks for agreeing to talk with me. *(shake hands all round as soldiers give their real names. All sit down on side benches)* I have just arrived in Afghanistan and I know you are all soldiers, and that you're used to following orders and not speaking out of line, but let me ask you a question – and please give me the straight goods: What in heck are we doing in this baking hot country where the dust is so thick you could slice it with a knife?

Afghan 1: Well Ms. Blatchford, if you want to know *why* we're here, you'll have to ask the politicians back in Canada. They sent us here, and they're the ones who'll decide when we leave.

Christie: I might just do that! In the meantime, would you tell about some of the things we've been doing here on a regular basis?

Afghan 2: We do a lot of things actually Ms. Blatchford – just like we're trained to do.

Afghan 3: Our primary objective is to defeat the Taliban.

Afghan 2: We fight the Taliban and the Al-Qaeda terrorists who support them, but we also build schools, dams, provide medical care, and train Afghan soldiers and police so that one day they can take over when we leave.

Afghan 1: For the past couple of months our unit has been removing land-mines.

Christie: Maybe you could explain to our readers what land mines are?

Afghan 1: Land-mines – or Improvised Explosive Devices – are bombs that are buried in the earth, so that when people or vehicles or tanks walk or drive over them they explode.

Afghan 2: They can be as small as a hockey puck or as large as a kid's knapsack. They can blow off a kid's foot or destroy a truck full of troops. Most of our soldiers who have been killed in Afghanistan have been killed by land-mines.

Afghan 2: We find them on roads, in school yards, and in farmer's fields.

Christie: I know that your tour of duty is almost over. What do you think are some of the best things you've done here?

Afghan 1: For me, the best thing we've done is to help kids get back to school – especially the girls. The Taliban doesn't believe that girls should get an education, or that women are worthy of respect. There are some girls here – and young women too – who have never been to school because of the Taliban.

Afghan 2: For me, its when you see the little kids running around and laughing and forgetting they're in the middle of a war. It makes me think of my own kids, and how lucky we are to have good food to eat, clean water to drink, and schools to give them homework – just kidding. I know we're doing a good job here: just ask the kids!

Christie: Thank you all very much. I'll be sure to tell your stories to Canadians. Thanks for all you've done.

Musical Interlude: Your choice. *Curtains close.*

SCENE 4: *HOW DO WE MAKE PEACE IN OUR WORLD?*

Narrator 1: It's clear that being a United Nations peacekeeper – or a peacemaker – is a tough job.

Narrator 2: But it's a job that Canada's soldiers, sailors, and air force have done willingly since 1956.

Narrator 2: Sometimes the United Nations and NATO has asked Canada to put our military in the middle of some pretty awful war zones. And if we had to do some fighting, we were ready for it.

Narrator 1: But as much as possible, we always try to do the least amount of harm and the most amount of good. What does that mean in choices?

Narrator 2: It means being involved.

Narrator 1: It means walking a middle line, even when there doesn't seem to be one.

Narrator 2: And being a positive influence in the face of major disagreements, by listening well and finding creative solutions.

Narrator 1: Sometimes it means building and even rebuilding.

Narrator 2 It always means staying involved and standing up for peace.

Narrator 1: That's what *peacekeepers* do. That's what *peacemakers* do. What can *WE* do? Let's go back to our own lives.

Curtain opens. All three groups are on the stage in tight frozen tableau groupings. Each group is returned to the point of discord. The re-enact the scene in the "better" way of response, and then freeze.

Narrator: How do you make peace in your family?

Family Scene:

Parent 1: (*Comes in the door.*) I'm home! Hello everyone. Were you able to pick up my shirts from the dry cleaners today?

Parent 2: Oh, I'm so sorry, I forgot. I had to stop at the bank and pick up groceries for supper and I just....

Parent 1: Don't worry about it. I know you're busy at work. It was just a favour.

Parent 2: I can get it after supper if you like.

Parent 1: Why don't we go together? I'm returning some new running shoes I bought that I don't really need. And then maybe we could all go to the library.

Parent 1: That's a good idea. (*Freeze tableau as they smile at each other*)

Child 1: I don't want to watch that show!

Child 2: You don't? What would you rather watch?

Child 1: I don't know really, but you got to choose last time.

Child 2: Okay, why don't we find something we both want to watch?

Child 1: I've got a better idea! (*flicks the clicker a few times*) Why don't we turn off the TV and play a game instead?

Child 2: Good idea!

Grandparent: It's so nice without the TV on. I can finally think straight. Why don't we play a hand of cards together?

Child 3: Hey, that's my favourite t-shirt you're wearing.

Child 2: Sorry .... I should have asked.

Child 3: I would appreciate it next time if you did. But since you loan me your iPod all the time I don't mind.

Child 2: Sorry, I'll be sure to ask you next time.

Parents: I love it when we're all home! It's so peaceful!

Narrator: Now *that's* how you make a family of peace.

(*Freeze*)

Playground Scene:

Ball Player: You want the ball? ... you can have it! (*throws it nicely*)

New Kid: (*catching it*) Thanks! Why do I get to go first?

Ball Player: It's just something we do to new kids around here.

(*Freeze*)

Chanters: Salute to the captain, bow to the queen;
Turn your back on the dirty submarine.
I can do the heel-toe; I can do the splits.
I can do the wiggle-waggle just like this!
(*All three wiggle-waggle.*)

Teeter-Totters: (*gesturing at the Chanters*) Look at them!

Ball Players: Hey! How do you do that? (*They start imitating the "wiggle waggle."*)

Chanters: Salute to the captain, bow to the queen;
Turn your back on the dirty submarine.
I can do the heel-toe; I can do the splits.
I can do the wiggle-waggle just like this!
(*All three wiggle-waggle.*)

Teetor-Totters: That looks ... strange!
It's no stranger than going up and down on a teeter-totter.
I suppose.
Maybe we can try it.
They'd probably let us play if we ask.

Ball Players: Don't you think that's weird?
It doesn't matter to me.
It looks like they're having fun.

(*New Kid's ball rolls away.*)

Teeter-Totters: Oops. here's your ball.

New Kid: Thanks. WOW! You kids are really nice!

Narrators: That's *how* you make a playground of peace.

Community Protest Scene:

Protester: What do we need?

Group: Change!
When do we need it?
Now!
What do we need?
Water Protection
When do we need it?
Now!
What do we need?
Change!
When do we need it?
Now!

Bystander 1: What's going on officer?

Police Officer: It's just a demonstration Miss.

Bystander 2: What could they possible be protesting?

Police Officer: They want the government to review the laws protecting Canadian waters from being sold off or polluted.

Bystander 2: Don't we live beside the biggest fresh water lakes in the world?

Bystander 1: Well, yes we do, but we've dumped a lot of chemicals and pollutants into them over the years.

Bystander 2: Listen, my generation needs jobs more than we need water – we should be using our resources to create more jobs and stop worrying about water.

Police Officer: That's your opinion, and you've got the right to it. And they have the right to voice their opinion too.

Bystander 2: Yes, I suppose that's correct Officer.

Bystander 2: Well, I don't really understand what your cause is. Maybe you could explain it to me?

Protester: Sure, here, read this pamphlet. It sums it up pretty good! Then, who knows, maybe you'd be interested in joining us?

Bystander 2: Yeah, who knows?

(*Freeze*)

Narrators: (*Stepping forward*) This is how you make a community of peace ...

All actors in scenarios together: ... and this is how we keep the peace.

Curtains close

Choir: *"Let There Be Peace on Earth"* by Jill Jackson and Sy Miller or *"Une Columbe"* sung by Celine Dion.

SCENE 5: *THE CEREMONY OF REMEMBRANCE*

*Curtains open onto the stage set with a Commonwealth War Graves Commission style headstone. The actors stand evenly spaced, two on one side and two on the other across the front of the stage. See **Teacher's Guide: Ceremony of Remembrance** for additional details and procedures.*

Narrator 1: Whenever we think about peace, we should think about November 11, and what it stands for. Today is the day when we remember the men and women who helped shape our country – and our world – by their participation in war and peacemaking.

Pearson: As Lester B. Pearson said in his acceptance speech for the Nobel prize, "(Hu)man(ity) has conquered outer space. He has not conquered himself. In the end, the whole problem always returns to people; yes, to one person and his own individual response to the challenges that confront him." *We hope that we will respond fully and fairly to the challenges confronting us now and in the future.

Narrator 2: We say thank you to those who respond to the call of their leaders and fought valiantly and selflessly.

Actor: We remember with affection and sadness those who were cut down in the promise of their youth or the richness of their middle years.

Narrator 1: We say thank you to all these Canadians who went before, whose contribution to the cause of freedom through two World Wars, the Korean War, and several United Nations Peacekeeping and UN sanctioned NATO missions forged a direction for our country and the world today.

Pearson: We remember the terrible cost of war. Let us use that knowledge to guide us towards peace.

Together: Together we remember. And we say thank you.

The Honour March takes place which is solemn but moving, like "*Hymn to the Fallen*" from the movie "*Private Ryan*."

Once the wreathe is laid that same person asks the audience to

"PLEASE STAND"

- **BUGLE CALL: The Last Post**

- **MOMENT OF SILENCE**

- **The moment of Silence is ended when the wreathe layer says, "Please join us in the singing of 'O Canada'."**

- **All sing "O Canada."**

Curtains close. The performance and the Ceremony of Remembrance is ended.

* Full text of Pearson's Nobel Peace Prize acceptance speech, and a one minute sound recording is available at Nobleprize.org

SELECTED BIBLIOGRAPHY FOR CLASSROOMS

World War I:

- Brewster, Hugh. *At Vimy Ridge: Canada's Greatest World War I Victory.* Toronto: Scholastic Canada, 2006
- Debon, Nicolas. *A Brave Soldier.* Toronto: A Groundwood Book, 2002.
- Granfield, Linda. *In Flanders Fields.* Toronto: Fitzhenry and Whiteside, 1995.
- Granfield, Linda. *Where Poppies Grow.* Toronto: Fitzhenry and Whiteside, 2001.
- Livesay, Robert and A.G. Smith. *The Great War.* Fitzhenry and Whiteside: Markham, Ontario, 2006.

World War II:

- Brewster, Hugh. *On Juno Beach.* Toronto: Scholastic Canada Ltd., 2005.
- Brewster, Hugh. *Dieppe: Canada's Darkest Day of WWII.* Toronto: Scholastic Canada Ltd, 2009.
- McCann, Michelle R. *Luba, the Angel of Bergen-Belsen.* Berkeley, California: Tricycle Press, 2003.
- Renaud, Anne. *A Bloom of Friendship: The Story of the Canadian Tulip Festival.* Montreal: Lobster Press, 2004.
- Panchyk, Richard. *World War II for Kids.* Chicago: Chicago Review Press, 2002.

Korean War:

- Balgassi, Haemi. *Peacebound Trains.* New York: Clarion Books, 1996.

Peacekeeping:

- Peace Child International. *Stand Up, Speak Out: A Book About Children's Rights, written by young people around the world.* London: Peace Child International, 2002.
- Scholes, Katherine. *Peace Begins With You.* Boston: Sierra Club Books by Little, Brown and Company, 1989. *Special Acknowledgment for ideas on conceptualizing the idea of "peace" to younger children.*
- Winter, Jonah. *Peaceful Heroes.* Arthur A. Levine Books: New York, 2009.

Combined Resources:

- MacLeod, Elizabeth. *The Kids Book of Canada At War.* Toronto: Kids Can Press, 2007.
- Useful websites and free materials for educators include: **Canadian War Museum, Library and Archives Canada, Veterans Affairs Canada, Canadian Legion, Historica – Dominion Institute** (especially the "Memory Project.") and **Foreign Affairs and International Trade Canada.**

RESEARCH BIBLIOGRAPHY

- Allen, Ralph. *"Letter From France"* in *Globe and Mail,* June 12, 1944.
- Barris, Ted and Alex Barris. *Days of Victory: Canadians Remember 1939-1945.* Toronto: Macmillan Canada, 1995.
- Barris, Ted. *Deadlock in Korea.* Macmillan Canada; Toronto, 1999.
- Benedict, Michael (editor). *Canada at War: from the archives of Maclean's.* Toronto: Viking Press, 1997.

- Bercuson, David J. *Blood on the Hills: The Canadian Army in the Korean War*. Toronto: University of Toronto Press, 1999.
- Berton, Pierre. *Marching As to War; Canada's Turbulent Years 1899-1953*. Toronto: Random House of Canada, 2001.
- Blatchford, Christie. "Pitching a long view of Afghan mission". *Globe and Mail,* September 2006.
- Blatchford, Christie. "The dogs of war". *Globe and Mail,* Saturday 22, 2006. pg. A 13.
- Borda, Jenifer. *War and Peacekeeping: Primary Documents of 29th Century Canada*. Oakville Ontario: Rubicon Publishing, 2002.
- Broadfoot, Barry. *Six War Years, 1939-1945*. Toronto: Doubleday Canada Ltd., 1974.
- Cohen, Andrew. *While Canada Slept: How we lost our place in the world*. McClelland and Stewart.: Toronto, 2003.
- Cook, Tim. *At the Sharp End: Canadians Fighting the Great War 1914-1916*, Volume One. Toronto: Viking Canada, 2007.
- Copp, Terry. *Fields of Fire: The Canadians in Normandy*. Toronto: University of Toronto Press, 2003.
- Dewar, Jane *(selected by, from the pages of Legion Magazine)*. *True Canadian War Stories*. Toronto: Prospero Books, 1986.
- Giesler, Patricia. *Valour Remembered: 1) Canada and the First World War, 2) Canada and the Second World War, 3) Canadians in Korea*. Government of Canada: Veterans Affairs, 1982.
- Granatstein, J.L. and Desmond Morton. *A Nation Forged in Fire: Canadians and the Second World War, 1939-1945*. Toronto: Lester & Orpen Dennys, 1989.
- Granatstein, J.L. and Douglas Lavender. *Shadows of War, Faces of Peace: Canada's Peacekeepers*. Toronto: Key Porter Books, 1992.
- Gwyn, Sandra. *Tapestry of War*. Toronto: Harper Collins Publisher Ltd., 1992.
- Kipp, Sgt. Charles D. *Because We Are Canadians*. Toronto: Douglas and McIntyre. 2003.
- Leach, Norman S. *Canadian Peacekeepers: Ten Stories of Valour in War-Torn Countries*. Calgary, Alberta: Folklore Publishing, 2005.
- Morton, Desmond and J.L. Granatstein. *Marching to Armageddon: Canadians and the Great War 1914-1919*. Toronto: Lester and Orpen Dennys Ltd.,1989.
- Pearson, Lester B. Mike: *The Memoirs of the Right Honourable Lester B. Pearson/Volume One, Two, and Three*. Toronto: University of Toronto Press. 1972 (Volume One), 1973 (Volume Two), 1975 (Volume Three).
- Ruck, Calvin W. *The Black Battalion, 1916 -1920 Canada's Best Kept Military Secret*. Nimbus Publishing Limited: Halifax, Nova Scotia, 1987. (*for the story of Jeremiah Jones, pg. 25*)
- Saul, John Raulston. *A Fair Country:Telling Truths About Canada*. Toronto: Viking Group. 2008
- Saunders, Doug. "Contingent of One" in the *Globe and Mail,* Saturday May 20, 2006.Section F1-5.
- Watson, Brent Byron. *Far Eastern Tour; The Canadian Infantry in Korea*, 1950-1953. Montreal: McGill-Queen's University Press, 2002.
- Wilson Janet. One Peace: *True Stories of Young Activists*. Victoria, B.C. Orca Book Publishers, 2008.

ACKNOWLEDGEMENTS

- Michael O'Keeffe, outstanding editor, whose commitment and discerning ear for dialogue and eye for detail made all the difference.

- Jane Burton, who established the rich and moving Remembrance Day Play and Ceremony tradition at Fisher Park and Summit Alternative Public School, and left the framework for me to follow! Dale Hayward, who had faith in my plays and produced them.

- For a deep source of inspiration and love: Michael O'Keeffe, husband; our children Aidan and Kathleen; and our extended family who lived through both war and peace; Erika (nee Schlotmann) Brockmann – a childhood in wartime; Tony Brockmann – a peacekeeper in Cyprus, 1964; Uncle George Brockmann – a Canadian soldier in Europe in WWII; Patrick O'Keeffe – an RAF wireless operator in WWII; Erich Schlotmann and James O'Keeffe – soldiers on opposing fronts in WWI.

- Harry Martin of the Canadian War museum, whose timely knowledge and loan of authentic costumes through the "Living History" program added so much to previous productions.

- Administrators Denis Delorme, Francesse Kopczweski, Trudy Brand-Jacobson, Kathi Kay, and John Sainis, for their active support of the Remembrance Day endeavour through the years and productions.

- Colleagues and volunteers, too numerous to mention, whose talents in choir, dance, costume, sound, lighting, and assistant directing made these productions a joyful ensemble effort.

- Students from Fisher Park Public School, Summit Alternative Public School and Rockcliffe Park Public School, Ottawa who have acted, sang, danced or assisted in the plays and made the pathos of the past, live.

- Photography: mostly Michael O'Keeffe and Barbara Brockmann. Front cover (Michael O'Keeffe) clockwise from far left: Brian Brockmann, Bethany McKinley-Young, Jimmy Knotsch Papatsie, Chelsea Okankwu, Ethan McKinley-Young, Aidan O'Keeffe, Olivier Makuch, Centre: Kathleen O'Keeffe.

- To those who lived the stories this theatre tells THANK YOU.